THE ULTIMATE BOOK OF
ANIMALS

Claudia Martin

Consultant: Jules Howard

ARCTURUS

ARCTURUS

Author: Claudia Martin
Designer: Lorraine Inglis
Picture research: Paul Futcher
Consultant: Jules Howard
Editor: Becca Clunes
Design manager: Jessica Holliland
Managing editor: Joe Harris

ISBN: 978-1-3988-1535-3
CH007796NT
Supplier 13, Date 0822, PI 00000667

Printed in China

THE ULTIMATE BOOK OF
ANIMALS

CONTENTS

INTRODUCTION

Around 665 million years ago, the first simple animals lived in the ocean. Today, scientists have named 1.5 million living species of animals, but believe there may be over 5.5 million more to be discovered. The largest species is the blue whale, 33.6 m (110 ft) long. The smallest is a myxozoan, 0.0085 mm (0.0003 in) long, which lives inside fish.

Scientists who study animals are called zoologists. When trying to discover more about an animal, they first study its body shape and features. By looking closely at an animal's teeth, claws, fur, scales, fins, or wings, they find out about how it hunts, hides, moves, and mates. Zoologists study how an animal's features are useful in its particular habitat, whether that is a coral reef, a rain forest, or the frozen surface of the Arctic Ocean. On the African savanna, a giraffe's extremely long neck enables it to reach into tall trees to eat twigs, while shorter plant-eaters such as kudu and impala feed below. On shallow lakes and marshes, a swan's long neck is useful for picking underwater plants as it paddles at the surface.

Zoologists also study how animals interact with others in their species, with different species, and with their environment. For example, beavers mate with one partner for life. The pair care for their babies, which may stay with their parents for many years, helping them care for younger babies. Together, the family builds dams across rivers and lakes, by chewing down trees with their strong front teeth. These dams create a pond for the beaver family to live in. Beaver ponds are also an important habitat for many other animal species, including turtles, water voles, otters, trout, snails, mussels, dragonflies, bark beetles, and ducks. Aside from humans, no animal species has a greater effect on its environment.

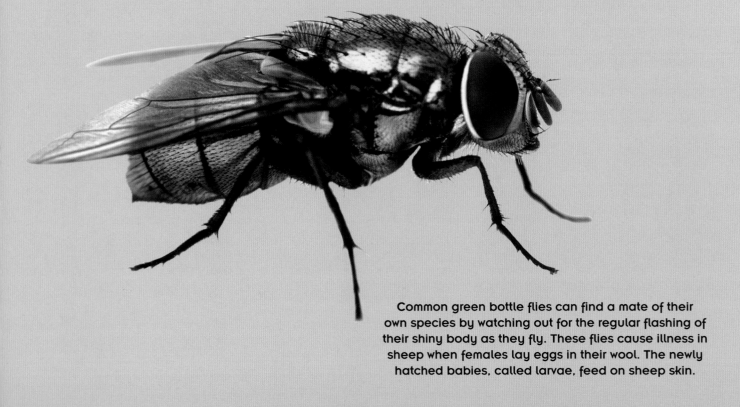

Common green bottle flies can find a mate of their own species by watching out for the regular flashing of their shiny body as they fly. These flies cause illness in sheep when females lay eggs in their wool. The newly hatched babies, called larvae, feed on sheep skin.

Up to 5.7 m (18.7 ft) tall, giraffes live in woodlands and in the tree-dotted grasslands of the African savanna.

Chapter 1

THE WORLD OF ANIMALS

From tiny ants to roaring lions, all animals share key characteristics. All animals must feed on other living things. Nearly all animals need to take in oxygen. At some point in their life, all animals can move.

Unlike plants, which make food from sunlight, animals cannot produce their own food. To supply their body with energy for living, growing, and reproducing, animals eat other living things. In addition, nearly all animals need water, which is used for body processes and carrying materials around the body.

Every animal is made of tiny building blocks called cells. The smallest animals, such as myxozoans, have fewer than a thousand cells, but most animals have trillions. With very few exceptions, animals need oxygen, which cells need to turn food into energy they can use. Without that energy, cells—and animals—would die. Land-living animals take oxygen from air using lungs, while many water-dwelling animals take it from water using special structures called gills or by soaking it up through their skin.

Although some animals, such as sponges and corals, become sessile (non-moving) as adults, all animals can move at some point in their life, over or through land, in the air, or in water. Finally, nearly all animals reproduce by mating, usually between male and female members of the same species. A few, such as cnidarians, reproduce by another method, such as by creating copies of themselves.

Linnaeus's two-toed sloths move very slowly and only when necessary. Their stillness prevents them being spotted by hawks and jaguars.

Diets

Animals eat other living things, including animals, plants, or simpler creatures such as algae, bacteria, and fungi. Some animals, called carnivores, eat other animals, including mammals, fish, and insects. Carnivores often have sharp teeth, crushing jaws, or sucking mouthparts. Herbivores eat plant material such as leaves, fruit, or bark. Some herbivores have more than one stomach so they can extract as much energy as possible from plants. Omnivores eat a mixture of animal and plant or other material. The benefit of being an omnivore is being able to find food in a changeable or challenging environment.

The Atlantic puffin is a carnivore, diving into the ocean to catch fish such as sand eels.

While some animals spend most of their life alone, ants live in large groups, called colonies. These army ants have built a bridge with their own bodies, so other members of the colony can cross.

ANIMAL GROUPS

Scientists divide animals into six large groups, based on their shared characteristics: mammals, birds, amphibians, reptiles, fish, and invertebrates. Within these groups, animals are divided into smaller and smaller groupings of increasingly similar animals, ending with a species. A species is made up of animals that look very similar and can mate together.

Mammal

A mammal grows hair at some point during its life. It has lungs for breathing air. A female mammal feeds her babies on milk that she makes in her own body.

Kingdom:	Animalia (Animals)
Subphylum:	Vertebrata (Animals with a backbone)
Class:	Mammalia (Mammals)
Order:	Carnivora (Sharp-toothed meat-eaters)
Family:	Herpestidae (Mongooses)
Species:	*Suricata suricatta*

Meerkat

Stork-billed kingfisher

Bird

A bird has feathers, wings, a toothless beak, and a lightweight skeleton. It breathes air using lungs.

Kingdom:	Animalia (Animals)
Subphylum:	Vertebrata (Animals with a backbone)
Class:	Aves (Birds)
Order:	Coraciiformes (Raven-like birds)
Family:	Alcedinidae (Kingfishers)
Species:	*Pelargopsis capensis*

Reptile

A reptile has skin covered by scales or bony plates called scutes. It has lungs for breathing air.

Kingdom:	Animalia (Animals)
Subphylum:	Vertebrata (Animals with a backbone)
Class:	Reptilia (Reptiles)
Order:	Crocodilia (Crocodiles)
Family:	Gavialidae (Thin-snouted crocodiles)
Species:	*Gavialis gangeticus*

Gharial

Amphibian

An amphibian usually starts life in freshwater, using gills to take oxygen from water, then grows lungs for breathing air and living on land.

Kingdom:	Animalia (Animals)
Subphylum:	Vertebrata (Animals with a backbone)
Class:	Amphibia (Amphibians)
Order:	Anura (Frogs)
Family:	Ranidae (True frogs)
Species:	*Pelophylax lessonae*

Pool frog

Daisy parrotfish

Fish

A fish usually has fins and scale-covered skin. It lives in water and takes in oxygen using gills.

Kingdom:	Animalia (Animals)
Subphylum:	Vertebrata (Animals with a backbone)
Class:	Actinopterygii (Ray-finned fish)
Order:	Labriformes (Fleshy-lipped fish)
Family:	Scaridae (Parrotfish)
Species:	*Chlorurus sordidus*

Invertebrate

An invertebrate does not have a backbone. This huge group includes any animal not in the subphylum Vertebrata. Invertebrates may live on land or in water and have a range of methods of taking in oxygen.

Kingdom:	Animalia (Animals)
Phylum:	Arthropoda (Invertebrates with a tough covering)
Class:	Insecta (Insects)
Order:	Odonata (Dragonflies and damselflies)
Family:	Gomphidae (Club-tailed dragonflies)
Species:	*Ophiogomphus cecilia*

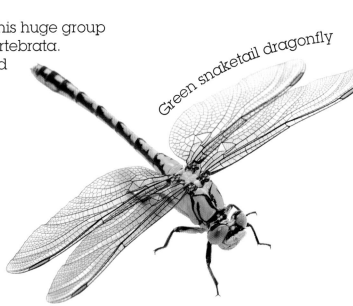
Green snaketail dragonfly

The Galápagos Islands' common cactus finch has a large, pointed beak, which is suited to reaching nectar and pollen from the flowers of prickly pear cacti.

EVOLUTION

Over thousands or millions of years, animals change their appearance and habits. This slow process, called evolution, has resulted in millions of species, which are all descended from early, ocean-dwelling animals.

The English scientist Charles Darwin (1809–82) was among the first to come up with a theory of evolution. He developed his ideas after studying animals in the Pacific Ocean's Galápagos Islands. He realized the islands' 18 species of finch were descendants of one species that had arrived on the islands millions of years ago. On different islands, the birds evolved different beak shapes to suit the available food, from cacti to insects.

Evolution depends on the fact that parents can pass on their characteristics—such as beak shape—to their babies. Characteristics are passed on through genes, which are instructions contained in cells. Within any species, there are slight differences in characteristics, so some birds may have stronger beaks than others. Useful characteristics, such as a stronger beak, give an individual a better chance of surviving long enough to reproduce. This means that useful characteristics stand a better chance of being passed on to the next generation, so they become more widespread.

In this way, simple ocean-dwelling animals evolved so that today's animals are adapted to countless environments, from deserts to caves and treetops. After a species has gone through significant changes, scientists call it an entirely new species.

Darwin noted the differently shaped shells of different species of Galápagos tortoise, with the Alcedo volcano tortoise's dome-shaped shell giving the tortoise's neck room to reach for low plants.

Family:	Thraupidae
Range:	Darwin's finches and other birds in the tanager family live in Central and South America
Habitat:	Forest, woodland, shrubland, and wetland
Diet:	Fruit, seeds, nectar, flowers, and insects
Size:	9–28 cm (3.5–11 in) long

White-eared conebill

Magpie tanager

HISTORY OF LIFE

The earliest animals were simple, spongelike invertebrates, which lived in the oceans around 665 million years ago. It was another 130 million years before the first animals with a backbone, called vertebrates, appeared.

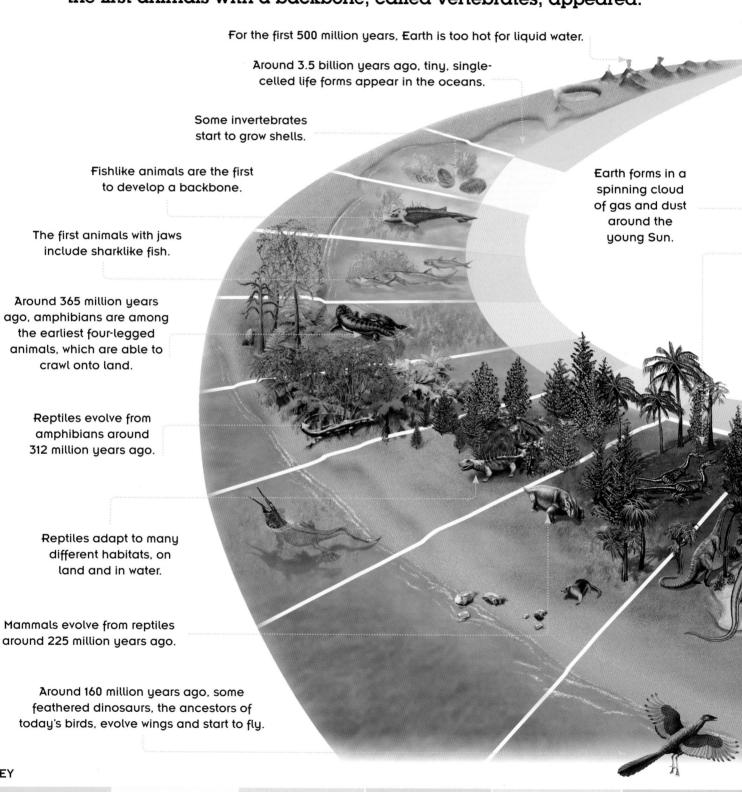

For the first 500 million years, Earth is too hot for liquid water.

Around 3.5 billion years ago, tiny, single-celled life forms appear in the oceans.

Some invertebrates start to grow shells.

Fishlike animals are the first to develop a backbone.

Earth forms in a spinning cloud of gas and dust around the young Sun.

The first animals with jaws include sharklike fish.

Around 365 million years ago, amphibians are among the earliest four-legged animals, which are able to crawl onto land.

Reptiles evolve from amphibians around 312 million years ago.

Reptiles adapt to many different habitats, on land and in water.

Mammals evolve from reptiles around 225 million years ago.

Around 160 million years ago, some feathered dinosaurs, the ancestors of today's birds, evolve wings and start to fly.

KEY

Precambrian Supereon	Cambrian Period	Ordovician Period	Silurian Period	Devonian Period	Carboniferous Period
4.5 billion years ago	541 million years ago	485 million years ago	444 million years ago	419 million years ago	359 million years ago

Clade:	Dinosauria
Range:	Dinosaurs lived on all continents
Habitat:	Forest, grassland, desert, swamp, rivers, and beaches
Diet:	Plants, invertebrates, fish, mammals, amphibians, and reptiles including other dinosaurs
Size:	40 cm–39.7 m (16 in–72 ft) long

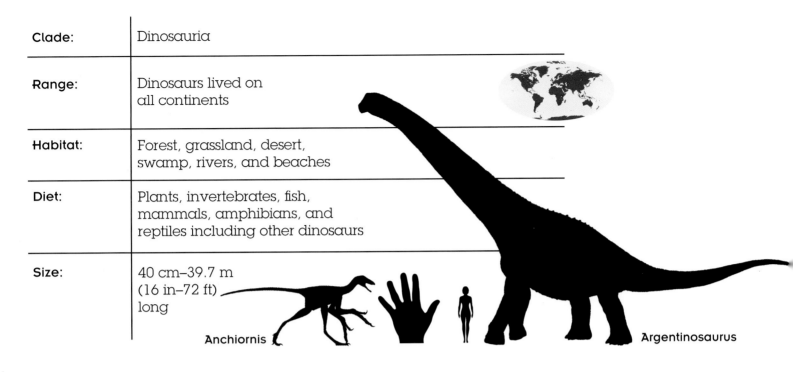

Anchiornis

Argentinosaurus

Around 233 million years ago, a group of land-living reptiles called dinosaurs evolve.

Dinosaurs dominate the land.

Tyrannosaurus, Triceratops, and all other dinosaurs are wiped out when an asteroid hits Earth around 66 million years ago.

Mammals dominate the land. Around 55 million years ago, large-brained mammals called primates, the ancestors of humans, evolve.

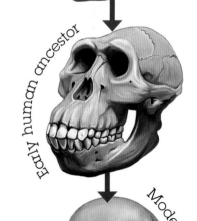

Primate skull

Early human ancestor

Around 350,000 years ago, modern humans evolve.

Modern human skull

Permian Period	Triassic Period	Jurassic Period	Cretaceous Period	Tertiary Period	Quaternary Period
299 million years ago	252 million years ago	201 million years ago	145 million years ago	66 million years ago	2.6 million years ago

HABITATS

An animal's habitat is its natural home. Each animal is suited to the amount of heat, light, and water of its habitat. Habitats may be vast, such as a rain forest, or as small as the rotting wood of a fallen tree.

Animals are adapted to their habitat, with body features and habits that help them survive. In polar regions, animals such as polar bears and penguins have deep layers of fat and thick fur or feathers to keep them warm. Animals that live in hot deserts are adapted to drinking little water. Some, such as scorpions, have a thick covering that stops them losing water to the air. Others, such as kangaroo rats, stay in burrows during the day so they do not overheat.

A region's large-scale habitats are dependent on its climate. Climate is affected by distance from the equator, where it is hot due to the Sun being overhead for longer periods of the year. Within every large-scale habitat, such as woodland, are numerous microhabitats, such as bark, flowers, leaf litter, and soil. Rotting wood may be home to hundreds of species of invertebrates, including carpenter ants, woodboring beetles, centipedes, and spiders.

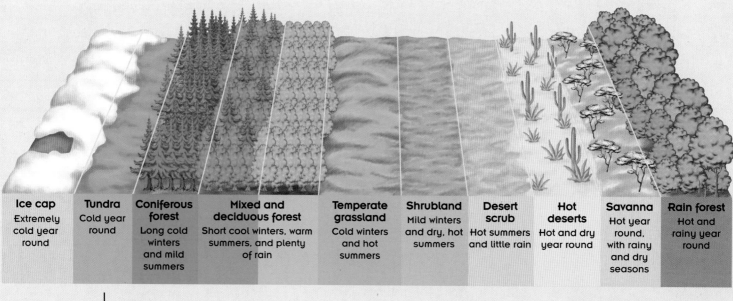

| **Ice cap** Extremely cold year round | **Tundra** Cold year round | **Coniferous forest** Long cold winters and mild summers | **Mixed and deciduous forest** Short cool winters, warm summers, and plenty of rain | **Temperate grassland** Cold winters and hot summers | **Shrubland** Mild winters and dry, hot summers | **Desert scrub** Hot summers and little rain | **Hot deserts** Hot and dry year round | **Savanna** Hot year round, with rainy and dry seasons | **Rain forest** Hot and rainy year round |

Family:	Ursidae
Range:	Bears live in Europe, Asia, and the Americas
Habitat:	Forest, grassland, tundra, and sea ice
Diet:	Leaves, fruit, roots, insects, fish, seals, and deer
Size:	1–3 m (3.3–9.8 ft) long

Sun bear   Polar bear

Trees grow in regions with plenty of rain. In northern regions with cold winters, most trees are coniferous, with needle-shaped leaves that can survive the long winter. Farther south, in temperate regions, which have cool winters and warm summers, many trees are deciduous, with broad delicate leaves that fall before the brief winter. On the tundra and ice cap, it is too cold for trees to grow.

The polar bear spends winter on the sea ice of the Arctic Ocean, where its pale coat helps with camouflage. Today, the sea ice is shrinking due to climate change. The burning of fuels such as coal, oil, and natural gas is releasing extra carbon dioxide, a gas that traps the Sun's heat, warming the air and oceans.

Up to 1 m (3.3 ft) tall, the sharp-beaked heron is near the top of the food chain in lakes and wetlands.

FOOD CHAINS

A food chain is a series of living things that eat each other. A food chain starts with a living thing, such as a plant, that produces its own food. It ends with an apex predator, such as a great white shark, that has no predators of its own.

All living things need energy. A food chain shows how energy is passed from one living thing to the next. The first link in all food chains is a producer. Producers may be plants, algae, bacteria, or archaea, which use the energy in sunlight or chemicals to make their own food energy. When producers are eaten, some of that energy is passed on.

Animals that eat producers are called primary consumers. Primary consumers may be eaten by bigger animals, known as secondary consumers, which may be eaten by even bigger animals, known as tertiary consumers. There are usually no more than five links in a food chain. Only about 10 percent of energy is passed on at each link in the chain, as the rest is used up by the animal's own body processes. This is why there are fewer apex predators, such as great white sharks, than there are primary consumers, such as shrimp. Great white sharks need to eat many smaller animals to survive.

Quaternary consumers

Tertiary consumers

Secondary consumers

Primary consumers

Producers

In this example of an ocean food chain, producers are eaten by tiny invertebrates, which are eaten by larger and larger fish, ending with a great white shark.

Family:	Ardeidae
Range:	Herons live on all continents except Antarctica
Habitat:	Edges of lakes, rivers, swamps, and oceans
Diet:	Fish, crabs, insects, lizards, and frogs
Size:	25–152 cm (10–60 in) long

Dwarf bittern   Goliath heron

LIFE CYCLES

Some animals are born from an egg, but others are born wriggling and alive from their mother's body. While many baby animals look similar to their parents, others go through significant body changes, called metamorphosis.

All mammals, apart from the five species of egg-laying monotremes, give birth to live young. Most fish and amphibians release jellylike eggs in water. The majority of reptiles and all birds lay shelled eggs on land. Most invertebrates also lay eggs, on land, in soil, or in water. However, a few fish, amphibians, reptiles, and invertebrates carry their developing young inside them. Some of these—such as great white sharks—are ovoviviparous, with eggs hatching inside the mother's body. Others—such as the common lizard—are viviparous, with the embryo (unborn baby) developing inside the mother's body, as in the case of mammals.

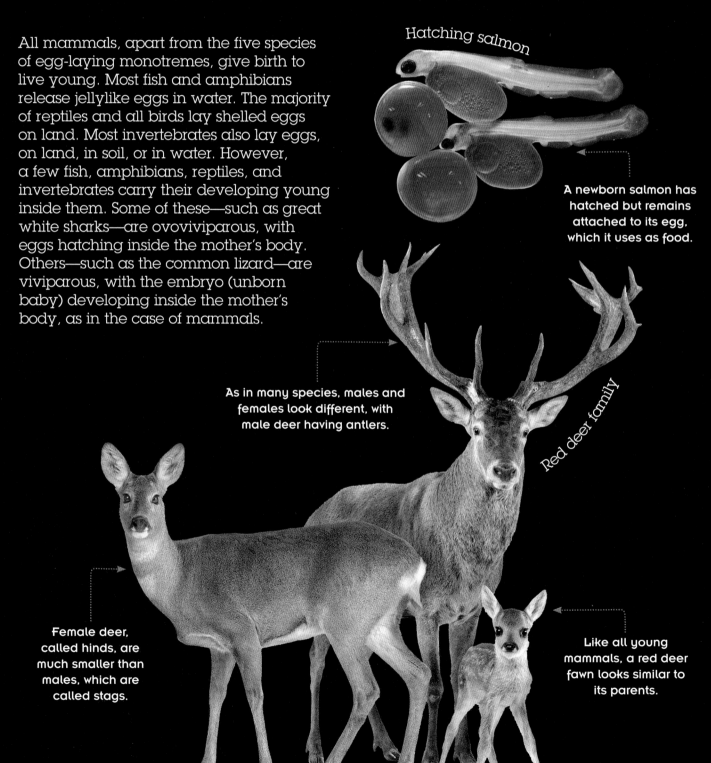

Hatching salmon

A newborn salmon has hatched but remains attached to its egg, which it uses as food.

As in many species, males and females look different, with male deer having antlers.

Red deer family

Female deer, called hinds, are much smaller than males, which are called stags.

Like all young mammals, a red deer fawn looks similar to its parents.

Some fish, most amphibians, and many invertebrates, including insects, go through metamorphosis. Metamorphosis involves not just body changes but also changes in habits, such as diet. The advantage of metamorphosis is that animals make use of different food sources and environments in their life, avoiding competition between adults and young.

Many insects go through four stages of metamorphosis: egg, larva, pupa, and adult. An insect hatches from an egg into a wormlike larva. To begin the pupa stage, the larva often builds itself a protective covering, inside which it develops adult body parts. Most amphibians go through a three-stage lifecycle: egg, larva, and adult.

It weaves a pupal case out of palm threads.

Life cycle of a red palm weevil

Like most insect larvae, the palm weevil larva feeds almost continuously. It eats the leaves and trunk of palm trees.

Among the shortest lifespans are those of common fruit flies, which live for just 50 days. The vertebrate with the longest life is probably the Greenland shark, which might live for 400 years. The longest-living animals of all may be invertebrates such as the immortal jellyfish, which can change back into its larval form if it is hurt.

Immortal jellyfish

This jellyfish might be able to change back into a larva forever, but it is likely to be eaten by a predator eventually.

The immortal jellyfish measures just 4.5 mm (0.18 in) across.

MIGRATION

Many animals make a long journey, usually at a particular time each year. Animals may migrate because of a change in the season, the need for food or water, or to find a suitable place to mate.

When temperatures fall, around 1,800 of the world's 10,000 bird species migrate to warmer climates to escape the winter cold. Changes in temperature are also felt in the oceans. Every winter, Caribbean spiny lobsters walk from coastal to warmer, deeper waters. Other movements are driven by changes in rainfall. As the season changes from wet to dry, 1.7 million wildebeest move across the African grasslands in search of water and fresh grass.

Once a year, salmon living in the Pacific Ocean swim as far as 1,400 km (900 miles) up a river, to find a spot with gravel in which to lay eggs and plenty of insects to feed young fish. Loggerhead sea turtles may swim almost 12,900 km (8,000 miles) to the beach where they were born, to lay their eggs in the sand.

While most migrations happen on a yearly cycle, some take place daily. In terms of the weight of animals that undertake it, the world's largest migration is a daily vertical one, from dark, deep ocean waters, where there are fewer predators, to surface waters, where there is more food due to sunlight feeding plants and algae. Animals that make this journey include shrimp, squid, jellyfish, and fish. They feed in surface waters during the relative safety of night, returning to deeper waters during the day.

The Arctic tern migrates between the Arctic Ocean coasts, during the northern summer, and the Antarctic coast, during the southern summer, giving it the longest annual journey of up to 90,000 km (56,000 miles).

Genus:	Connochaetes
Range:	Wildebeest live in southern Africa
Habitat:	Grassland, shrubland, and open woodland
Diet:	Grass and leaves
Size:	1.7–2.4 m (5.6–7.9 ft) long

Black wildebeest

Blue wildebeest

Every year, blue wildebeest risk drowning and Nile crocodile attacks as they migrate across Africa's Mara River.

ENDANGERED ANIMALS

Human activities have put over a third of known animal species at risk of extinction. Scientists classify an at-risk animal as vulnerable, which means its numbers are shrinking; endangered, which means it is likely to be extinct in the near future; or critically endangered, which means it is close to extinction in the wild.

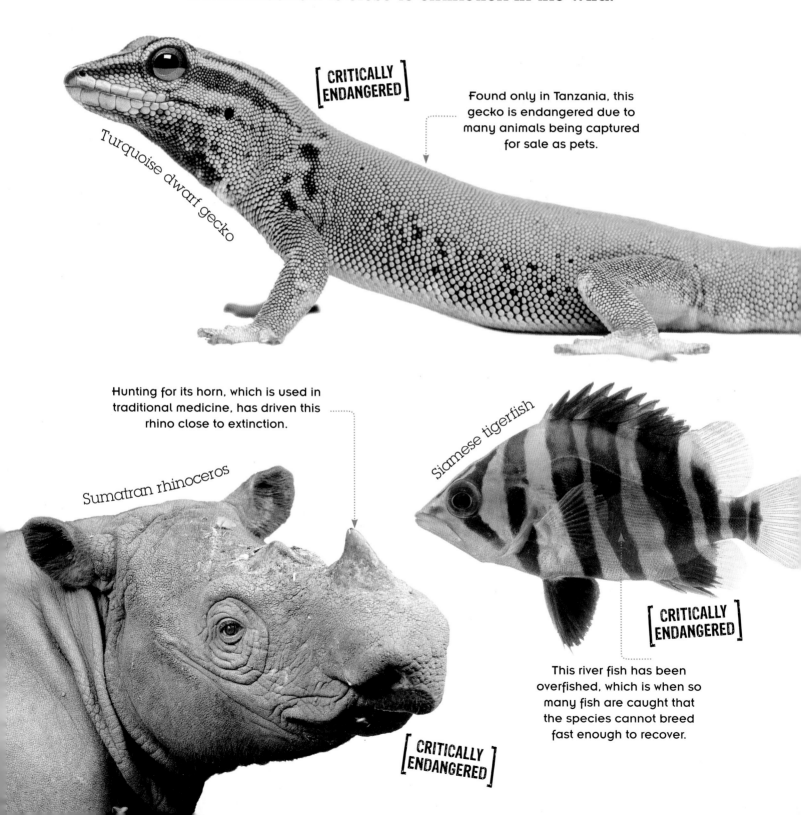

[CRITICALLY ENDANGERED]

Found only in Tanzania, this gecko is endangered due to many animals being captured for sale as pets.

Turquoise dwarf gecko

Hunting for its horn, which is used in traditional medicine, has driven this rhino close to extinction.

Siamese tigerfish

Sumatran rhinoceros

[CRITICALLY ENDANGERED]

This river fish has been overfished, which is when so many fish are caught that the species cannot breed fast enough to recover.

[CRITICALLY ENDANGERED]

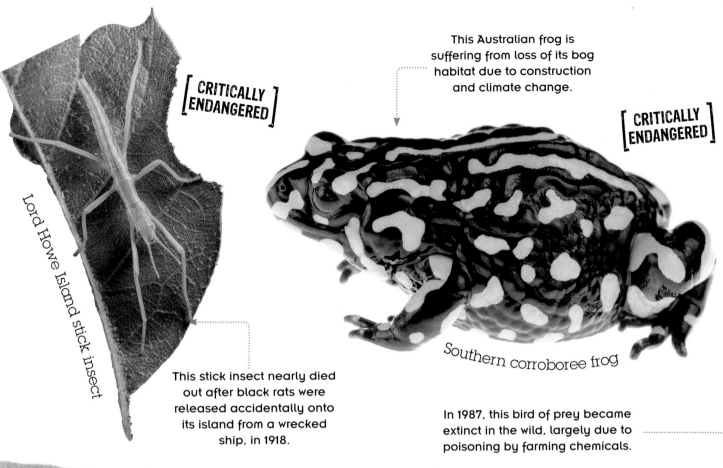

[CRITICALLY ENDANGERED]

Lord Howe Island stick insect

This Australian frog is suffering from loss of its bog habitat due to construction and climate change.

[CRITICALLY ENDANGERED]

This stick insect nearly died out after black rats were released accidentally onto its island from a wrecked ship, in 1918.

Southern corroboree frog

In 1987, this bird of prey became extinct in the wild, largely due to poisoning by farming chemicals.

California condor

After being bred in captivity, California condors were released into the wild again in 1991.

Family:	Cathartidae
Range:	New World vultures live in tropical, subtropical, and temperate regions of the Americas
Habitat:	Habitats from desert to rain forest, towns to mountains
Diet:	Carrion (animals found dead or dying), rotten fruit, and garbage
Size:	0.5–1.3 m (1.6–4.3 ft) long

Lesser yellow-headed vulture

Andean condor

[CRITICALLY ENDANGERED]

Descendants of the wild mouflon, sheep were domesticated around 12,000 years ago for their wool, meat, and milk.

DOMESTICATED ANIMALS

Domesticated animals have been tamed and kept by humans, often as a pet or on a farm. The first animal domesticated by humans, at least 15,000 years ago, was the wolf, the ancestor of today's pet dogs.

Many domesticated animals are farmed for their milk, meat, eggs, hair, or skin. The most common domesticated animal is the chicken, with over 25 billion alive today. Farm animals include mammals such as cows, pigs, and llamas; fish such as salmon; birds such as turkeys; reptiles such as crocodiles; and amphibians such as frogs. Some invertebrates are also farmed, including land snails, which are kept for food; western honey bees, which make honey; and silkworms, which produce silk.

Across the world, the most popular pets are dogs, followed by cats, hamsters, freshwater fish, mice, guinea pigs, and birds. While most dogs are kept only for companionship, some are trained to work with the police, in search and rescue, on farms, or with people who have illnesses or disabilities, such as blindness. Dogs that assist visually impaired people to avoid obstacles are called guide dogs.

When humans domesticate an animal, they take control not only of the animal's feeding and wellbeing but of its breeding. By selecting animals with particular characteristics to mate together, humans have developed different breeds with features such as laying many eggs, having long hair, or being gentle. Some strong, four-legged animals, such as horses and donkeys, have been bred for their ability to carry humans or loads.

Known for its drooping ears, the mini lop is a breed of domestic rabbit, which is descended from the wild European rabbit.

Species:	*Ovis aries*
Range:	Domestic sheep are farmed on all continents except Antarctica
Habitat:	Fields, grasslands, and hillsides
Diet:	Grass, hay, clover, weeds, and grain
Size:	0.8–1.6 m (2.6–5.2 ft) long

Ouessant sheep breed

Suffolk sheep breed

Chapter 2

MAMMALS

There are around 6,400 species of mammals, ranging in size from Kitti's hog-nosed bat, just 2.9 cm (1.1 in) long, to the blue whale, up to 29.9 m (98 ft) long. Mammals grow hair and breathe air using lungs. Mammal mothers feed their young with milk.

Mammals are in three groups: placentals, marsupials, and monotremes. Most mammals are placentals. Large groups of placentals include rodents, bats, primates (including monkeys and apes), and the mostly meat-eating carnivorans (including dogs, cats, and seals). Placental mothers give birth to live babies that are well developed. Marsupial mothers give birth to tiny, undeveloped young. Found only in Australasia, the five species of monotremes lay eggs.

Nearly all mammals have four limbs. Most mammals use all four for walking and running on land. In some mammals, the limbs have evolved to suit different lifestyles. Many monkeys have long arms suited to swinging through trees, while burrowing mammals such as prairie dogs have short, strong limbs. Water-living mammals, such as whales and seals, have limbs that have evolved into flippers. The front limbs of bats have become wings. A few mammals, including kangaroos and some species of ape, travel on their back limbs, by hopping or walking.

The short-beaked echidna is a monotreme. A female echidna lays a single rubbery-skinned egg in a burrow.

Hair

All mammals, even whales and dolphins, grow hair at some time in their life. Most mammals grow thick hair, called fur. This has oily guard hairs on top, for keeping out moisture, and thick underfur below, for staying warm or keeping sunlight off the skin. Many mammals have hair that is shaded to help with camouflage, from the patterned fur of cats to the white winter coat of the Arctic fox.

A skunk's coat is boldly patterned to warn predators that, if frightened, it will spray foul-smelling liquid. After a predator has been sprayed, it will remember not to approach a skunk again.

Like many mammals, golden snub-nosed monkeys live in groups. Two female monkeys are hugging each other as they care for a baby.

The red fox often lives in a pair with its mate, along with their young, called kits.

DOGS

The dog family includes pet dogs, wild dogs, wolves, foxes, and coyotes. Dogs usually have a long muzzle (combining its nose, mouth, and jaw), upright ears, and a bushy tail. They are meat-eaters, with differently shaped teeth suited to cutting flesh or grinding bones.

Most members of the dog family are social, which means they live together in families or larger groups, often called packs. African wild dogs form some of the largest packs, of up to 32 animals. These packs may hunt together, enabling the dogs to tackle animals much larger than themselves, such as wildebeest. The strongest and most experienced animals usually lead the pack.

Dogs communicate with each other using sounds, such as whines, growls, and barks. They also use body posture to show their intentions and needs. Aggressive wolves walk tall, use slow movements, and raise their hackles (the hair of their back and neck). Frightened wolves carry their bodies low, flatten their fur, and lower their tails. Dogs also use strong-smelling substances in their urine, or made in body parts called glands, to mark their territory and drive away rivals.

Pet dogs were bred from wolves, which were first tamed by humans around 15,000 years ago. By choosing which dogs to breed with each other, humans have developed different dog breeds with useful characteristics, such as gentleness or guarding.

The African wild dog's large, rounded ears can swivel to hear tiny sounds made by prey.

Family:	Canidae	
Range:	Wild members of the dog family live on all continents, apart from Antarctica	
Habitat:	Desert to tundra, mountains to forest, and cities to farmland	
Diet:	Small animals, such as mice and insects, to larger animals caught as a pack	
Size:	0.58–1.6 m (1.9–5.2 ft) long (for wild species)	Fennec fox Wolf

CATS

There are 37 species of cats, including the lion, jaguar, and domestic cat. These meat-eaters usually have sharp teeth, powerful jaw muscles, and curved retractile claws, which means they can be pulled back into the foot when not needed for slashing and pinning prey.

This Bengal tiger has an orange coat with dark stripes, offering camouflage in its shady forest habitat.

Tiger

The pointed canine teeth are ideal for piercing flesh.

Lion

The second largest species of cat, a lion is up to 2 m (6.6 ft) long.

The jaguar has large, forward-facing eyes that help it spot and chase prey.

Golden fur helps with camouflage in its dry grassland and woodland habitat.

Jaguar

Whiskers sense changes in air movement, giving the jaguar information about the shape and speed of nearby objects.

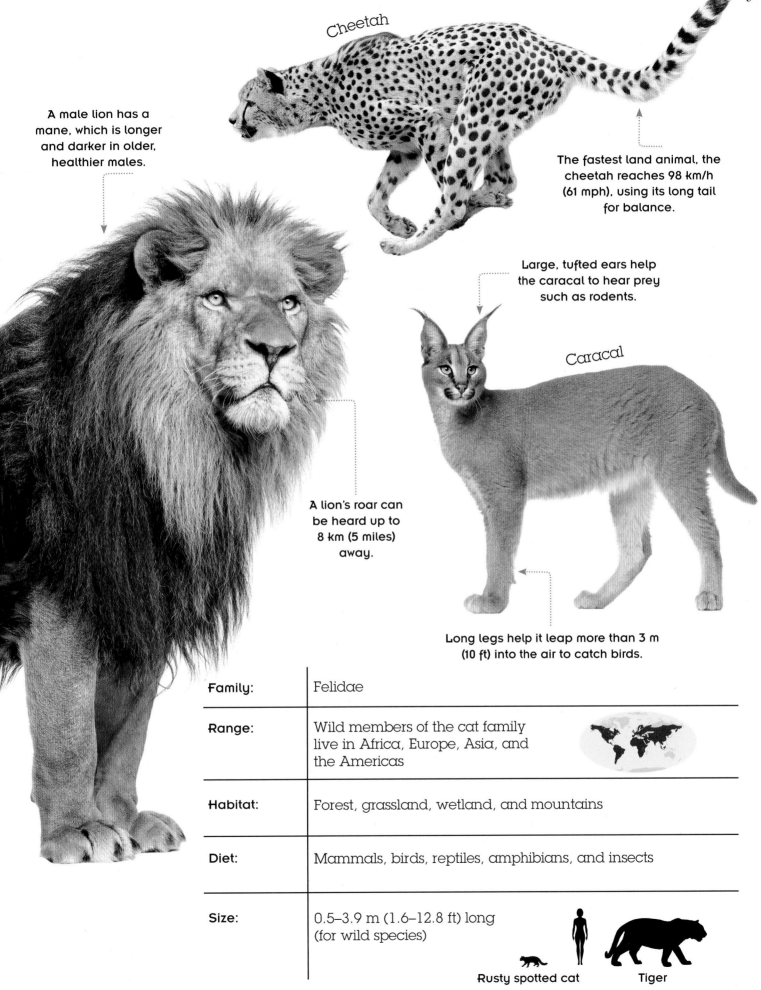

Cheetah

A male lion has a mane, which is longer and darker in older, healthier males.

The fastest land animal, the cheetah reaches 98 km/h (61 mph), using its long tail for balance.

Large, tufted ears help the caracal to hear prey such as rodents.

Caracal

A lion's roar can be heard up to 8 km (5 miles) away.

Long legs help it leap more than 3 m (10 ft) into the air to catch birds.

Family:	Felidae
Range:	Wild members of the cat family live in Africa, Europe, Asia, and the Americas
Habitat:	Forest, grassland, wetland, and mountains
Diet:	Mammals, birds, reptiles, amphibians, and insects
Size:	0.5–3.9 m (1.6–12.8 ft) long (for wild species)

Rusty spotted cat   Tiger

ELEPHANTS

The world's largest land animals, elephants weigh up to 6.9 tonnes (7.6 US tons), more than four average cars. There are three species: African bush elephants, African forest elephants, and Asian elephants. Elephants have a trunk, tusks, large ear flaps, and thick legs to hold their weight.

An elephant's trunk combines its nose and upper lip. Strong and heavily muscled, the trunk is used for grasping food, digging into soil for water, wrestling with other elephants, spraying water to keep cool, and covering the skin with dust or mud to block the harsh sun.

The tusks are the second incisors (front teeth) in the upper jaw, which grow throughout life, reaching up to 3 m (9.8 ft) long in African bush elephants. Some Asian elephants, particularly females, do not grow tusks. Tusks are used for fighting, digging for roots, and ripping bark from trees. Unfortunately, the tusks are made from ivory, which can be carved into ornaments. This has led to elephants being hunted for many centuries. Although trade in ivory is now banned, African bush and Asian elephants are endangered, while African forest elephants are critically endangered.

Elephants' large ear flaps help them to keep cool. Countless tiny blood vessels carry warm blood just below the skin of the ears, letting heat be lost to the air. Elephants also flap their ears to create a breeze.

This Asian elephant has smaller, rounder ears than an African elephant.

Family:	Elephantidae
Range:	African bush elephants live in Africa south of the Sahara Desert, African forest elephants in western Africa, and Asian elephants in southern Asia
Habitat:	African bush elephants and Asian elephants live in habitats from grassland to forest, while the African forest elephant lives in forests
Diet:	Grasses, roots, fruit, bark, and twigs
Size:	3–5 m (9.8–16.4 ft) long

African forest elephant

African bush elephant

An African bush elephant calf stays close to its mother. Females may remain with their mother all their life, but males leave the family group between the age of 10 and 19.

RODENTS

Rodents have four long, sharp front teeth, called incisors, that grow throughout their lives. By gnawing food, rodents wear down these teeth continually. Rodents are the most common mammals, with four out of every ten mammal species in the rodent order.

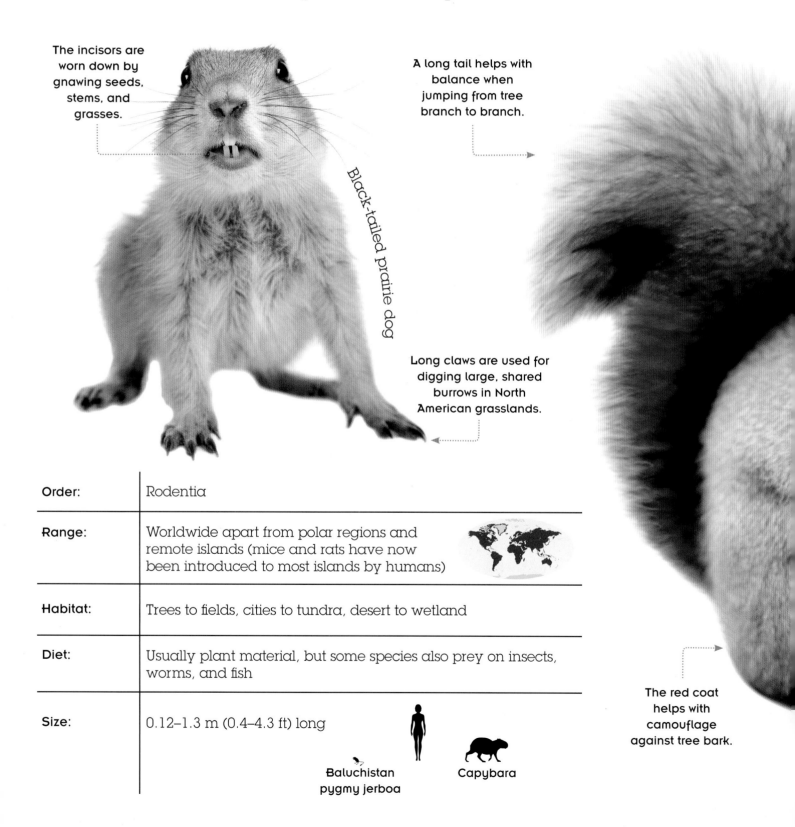

The incisors are worn down by gnawing seeds, stems, and grasses.

A long tail helps with balance when jumping from tree branch to branch.

Black-tailed prairie dog

Long claws are used for digging large, shared burrows in North American grasslands.

The red coat helps with camouflage against tree bark.

Order:	Rodentia
Range:	Worldwide apart from polar regions and remote islands (mice and rats have now been introduced to most islands by humans)
Habitat:	Trees to fields, cities to tundra, desert to wetland
Diet:	Usually plant material, but some species also prey on insects, worms, and fish
Size:	0.12–1.3 m (0.4–4.3 ft) long

Baluchistan pygmy jerboa

Capybara

Capybara

Unlike most rodents, a capybara does not have a tail.

Its toes are partly webbed (joined by skin) for paddling in swamps, lakes, and rivers.

Eurasian red squirrel

Thick fur is waterproofed with oil made in special glands.

The beaver chews down trees to build a dam, making a deep pond in which to live.

A large, paddle-like tail helps with swimming in rivers and lakes.

North American beaver

It eats seeds, nuts, berries, and shoots.

Eurasian harvest mouse

Its long tail can grip the stems of crops such as wheat and oats.

Sharp, curved claws help with climbing and holding food.

MARINE MAMMALS

Marine mammals rely on the ocean for food. Some, including whales and dolphins, spend all their life in water, coming to the surface to breathe air into their lungs. Others, such as seals and sea lions, split their time between water and coast.

Whales and dolphins make up a group of marine mammals called cetaceans. They are fully adapted to living in water, with their paddle-like tail, flipper-shaped front limbs, and smoothly shaped body. A female cetacean gives birth in the water to one baby, which she watches over closely. There are two groups of cetaceans: baleen whales, which filter tiny animals from the water using bristles in their mouth; and toothed whales, which catch fish and other swimming animals using their sharp teeth. The toothed whales include the animals we usually call dolphins.

Although a whale has mostly smooth skin so it can move easily through the water, sensitive hairs grow from fist-sized bumps.

Humpback whale

Seals, sea lions, and walruses are pinnipeds. They have a smoothly shaped body and four limbs shaped like flippers. They spend much of their life in water, but come to shore to give birth. On land, sea lions and walruses use all four limbs for walking. Seals spend less time on land than their relatives. They cannot pull their back limbs beneath their body to walk on them, so they wriggle along the ground.

Unlike a seal, a sea lion has ear flaps.

California sea lion

The humpback whale uses baleen bristles to catch tiny fish and krill.

The orca is the largest species of dolphin, reaching up to 8 m (26 ft) long.

Orca

Dolphins are toothed whales with cone-shaped teeth.

Common seal

Claws are used for holding and tearing squid and fish.

The kiang lives on the Tibetan Plateau at heights of 2,700–5,300 m (8,900–17,400 ft).

HORSES

Horses, donkeys, and zebras are members of the horse family. They are usually grazers, eating grasses and other low-growing plants. They have a long head, neck, and tail, as well as a mane of coarser hair that grows from the top of the neck. Each foot has a single toe with a tough covering called a hoof.

There are seven wild species in the horse family: three species of zebras, the kiang, the onager, the wild horse, and the African wild ass. Both the wild horse and African wild ass have been domesticated, or tamed and bred by humans. Donkeys are the descendants of domesticated African wild asses. Domestic horses range from miniature horses just 0.6 m (2 ft) tall to Shire horses 2.2 m (7.2 ft) tall. The only wild horse alive today is the endangered Przewalski's horse, found in the grasslands of Central Asia.

The kiang, onager, and African wild ass belong to the wild asses group, with long ears and the ability to survive in tough habitats such as deserts and windswept plateaus. They live in Asia and eastern Africa. Found only in Africa, zebras have black and white striped coats. Each zebra has its own unique pattern of stripes, which are believed to confuse biting flies by breaking up the zebra's outline so it is harder to land on. All members of the horse family live in a herd, which offers some protection from predators, as many eyes can watch for danger.

Unlike the domestic horse, a Grévy's zebra has a short mane that grows upright. It has a large tuft of hair at the end of a bony tail.

Family:	Equidae
Range:	Wild members of the family live only in Africa and Asia 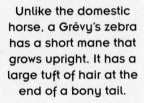
Habitat:	Woodland, grassland, desert, and mountains
Diet:	Usually grasses, as well as leaves, fruits, and roots
Size:	1.8–2.75 m (5.9–9 ft) long (for wild species)

Przewalski's horse   Grévy's zebra

APES

Apes are primates, which are mammals with large brains and hands capable of grasping. Unlike most primates, such as monkeys, apes do not have tails. Gibbons, orangutans, gorillas, chimpanzees, bonobos, and humans are all apes. Most apes, apart from humans, are threatened with extinction.

Bornean orangutan

Orangutans spend most of their time in trees.

The lips are used to make kissing and smacking noises to communicate.

Chimpanzee

Western lowland gorilla

A thick brow ridge helps to strengthen the skull.

The face, ears, hands, and feet are not covered by hair.

It can walk on two or four limbs, which it does by pushing off from its knuckles.

A chimpanzee's brain is around one-third the size of a human's, enabling it to use simple tools and work with members of its group.

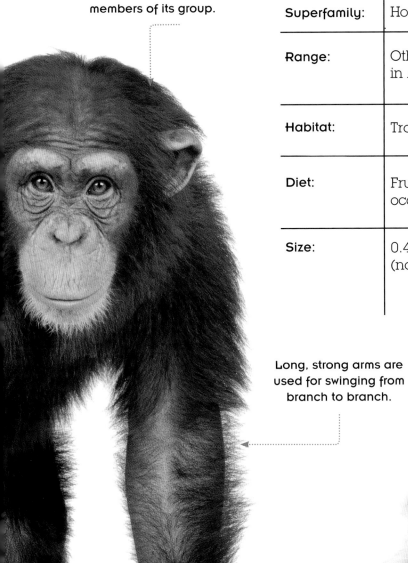

Superfamily:	Hominoidea
Range:	Other than humans, apes live in Africa and Southeast Asia
Habitat:	Tropical forest
Diet:	Fruit, roots, leaves, and occasionally meat
Size:	0.4–1.7 m (1.3–5.6 ft) long (not including humans)

Lar gibbon   Eastern gorilla

Long, strong arms are used for swinging from branch to branch.

Lar gibbon

It sings hooting songs with other members of its family.

Used for swinging quickly through the forest, its arms are much longer than its legs.

The big toes and thumbs are opposable, which means their tips can touch the tips of the other fingers or toes and be used for grasping.

MARSUPIALS

Marsupials are a group of mammals that give birth to babies which are tiny and undeveloped. The babies are usually carried in a pouch on their mother's body while they grow. The more than 300 species of marsupials live in Australasia and the Americas.

A marsupial mother is pregnant for just two to five weeks. When the baby, called a joey, is born, it is blind, furless, and around the size of a bumblebee. It crawls up its mother's body to a milk teat. The mother often licks her fur to leave a trail of scent for the joey to follow. Usually, the teat is inside a pouch, where the joey is warm and protected. While the joey develops fur and grows, it does not leave the pouch for several months. Then the joey starts to leave for short periods, but will return for up to a year.

The largest living marsupial, Australia's red kangaroo grows up to 2.8 m (9 ft) long.

The joey leaves the pouch for the last time after around 235 days.

Koala

Red kangaroo

Wombat

A koala joey leaves its mother's pouch after six months, but will hitch a ride on her back until a year old.

Rough palms and sharp claws help with climbing eucalyptus trees to find leaves to eat.

Sugar glider

Found in Australia, the sugar glider looks similar to the flying squirrel, a non-marsupial mammal.

Skin stretches between its front and back legs, enabling it to glide from branch to branch.

Marsupials started to evolve around 100 million years ago in the Americas, from where they spread to Australasia through Antarctica, which were joined at the time. Today, marsupials make up most of the native mammals in Australasia. Marsupials are as varied in their diet and habitats as other mammals. Many marsupials look similar to non-marsupial mammals, not because they are closely related but because they have evolved similar body shapes to survive in similar habitats.

Virginia opossum

This opossum is the only marsupial found in the United States.

Burrowing with its large front teeth and claws, the plant-eating wombat has evolved similarly to rodents.

BATS

There are over 1,400 species of bats. Although some mammals, such as sugar gliders, can glide on open wings, bats are the only mammals that can truly fly. Their wings are made of skin that stretches between extra-long finger bones and the body.

Most bats are nocturnal, hunting for food at night and spending the daylight hours roosting in caves, trees, or buildings. When roosting, bats hang upside down from their feet. Some bats eat fruit or the sweet nectar made by flowers, but the majority of bats eat insects. Some larger species eat bigger animals, such as lizards.

Three species of bats, known as vampire bats, feed only on the blood of mammals or birds. Vampire bats are found in the Americas, from Mexico to Argentina. When darkness falls, they seek out a sleeping animal, make a small bite in their skin, then lap up blood.

Insect-eating bats, vampire bats, and a few fruit-eaters use echolocation to find their way in the dark. These bats make very high-pitched sounds, which bounce off objects and return to the bat as an echo, enabling them to build up a "picture" of their surroundings. Some species have a fleshy extension on their nose, called a nose-leaf, which helps them to direct their echolocation calls.

Like all bats, the common pipistrelle has a short "thumb" claw at the front of its wing, which can be used for climbing.

Order:	Chiroptera
Range:	Throughout the world, apart from polar regions
Habitat:	Forest to desert, cities to farmland
Diet:	Insects or other small animals, fruit, nectar, or blood
Size:	2.9–30 cm (1 in–1 ft) long

Kitti's hog-nosed bat

Giant golden-crowned flying fox

The grey-headed flying fox lives in the forests of southeastern Australia, where it feeds on pollen, nectar, and fruit.

Chapter 3

BIRDS

Birds have wings, feathers, and a toothless beak. Their skeletons are lightweight, enabling most birds to fly. All birds lay hard-shelled eggs on land and breathe by drawing air into their lungs. There are around 10,000 species of birds, which are found on every continent.

Birds are the descendants of feathered dinosaurs, which lived 233 to 66 million years ago. Over millions of years, some dinosaurs' feathers grew longer and their front limbs evolved into wings, giving birds the ability to fly. Flying helps most birds to find food, escape predators, attract a mate, and—in many cases—make a yearly migration in search of suitable food or weather.

Feathers are made of a strong material called keratin, which is also found in birds' beaks and claws, reptile scales, and mammal hair. There are two main types of feathers. Long, strong-stalked "contour" feathers form the stiff, smooth outer layer of a bird's plumage. Contour feathers on the wings help a bird to power through the air. Underneath the contour feathers are shorter, fluffier "down" feathers, which keep the bird warm.

Female birds lay between 1 and 17 eggs at a time. Eggs must be kept safe and at a constant temperature until they hatch. Most birds lay their eggs in a nest. This may be built from materials such as mud, twigs, or grass. Some birds use a burrow or a hole in a tree.

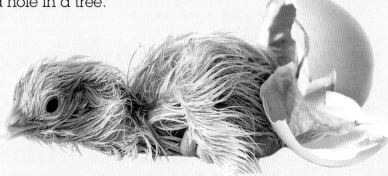

A newly hatched chicken climbs from its egg. Chicks have an egg tooth, a sharp bump on their beak, that they use to break through the shell.

Wings

A bird's wing shape is suited to its style of flight. Wide wings enable a bird to glide without flapping as it soars long distances in search of prey. The curved shape of the wing makes air pass faster over its top surface than below. This difference in air speed creates higher air pressure underneath the wing, which lifts the bird. Shorter wings are suited to fast, flapping flight.

The barn swallow (left) has short, pointed wings suited to flying fast and making sudden turns. With wings 2.4 m (7.9 ft) wide, the black-browed albatross glides over the oceans.

At mating time, a male blue-footed booby shows off his bright feet to a female in a foot-lifting dance.

HUMMINGBIRDS

These small birds feed on the sweet nectar made by flowers. They are known as hummingbirds because of the humming sound made by their wings beating rapidly through the air at up to 88 flaps per second. The world's smallest bird is the bee hummingbird.

To feed, a hummingbird extends its long beak and tongue into a flower while hovering in mid-air.

Broad-billed hummingbird

The male has a bright blue throat.

Violet sabrewing

A male berylline often chases other hummingbirds out of its territory.

These feathers are iridescent, seeming to change shade when seen at different angles, due to tiny bubbles that reflect the light differently.

Berylline hummingbird

Male hummingbirds are brighter than females, which helps them to attract a mate.

Rufous hummingbird

Like all hummingbirds, the rufous saves energy at night by entering a deep-sleep state, called torpor, with its breathing and heart beat slowing right down.

It spreads its tail feathers into a fan to help with stability while hovering.

A hummingbird's long beak has a shape suited to reaching into the particular flowers from which it feeds.

The feathers of its back shine metallic green.

Ruby-throated hummingbird

Females and young males have a dappled white throat.

The trumpet vine makes nectar to attract hummingbirds, which collect the flower's pollen on their feathers and carry it to another flower so it can grow new seeds.

Family:	Trochilidae
Range:	The Americas
Habitat:	Often tropical and subtropical forest, as well as woodland, mountains, and towns
Diet:	Nectar, insects, and spiders
Size:	5.5–23 cm (2–9 in) long

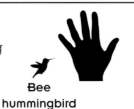

Bee hummingbird

Giant hummingbird

The keel-billed toucan has zygodactyl feet,
with two toes facing forward and two backward,
which are useful for grasping branches.

TOUCANS

There are more than 40 species of toucans, many of them with bright markings. Toucans have a large beak, often more than half the length of the bird's body. They use their beak for plucking fruit to eat as they sit on a tree branch.

Despite the beak's large size, it is very lightweight. It is not made of solid bone, but has struts of bone filled with spongey tissue. Without this adaptation, the beak would be too heavy for the bird to lift. In addition to feeding, a toucan uses its beak for fighting with other toucans, by hitting their beaks together. Toucans may fight to establish which birds are leaders in their flock or to impress a mate. They have more spare time than most birds, as the fruit they eat takes a long time to digest, leaving the bird with a full stomach and unable to feed again for over an hour after eating. Keel-billed toucans have also been seen using their beaks to throw food into each other's mouths.

Toucans nest in tree holes that formed naturally in old trees or that were made by another animal, such as a woodpecker.

A female usually lays two to four eggs in the nest, which hatch after two to three weeks. The newborn chicks are featherless and blind, so are brought food by both parents for their first six weeks.

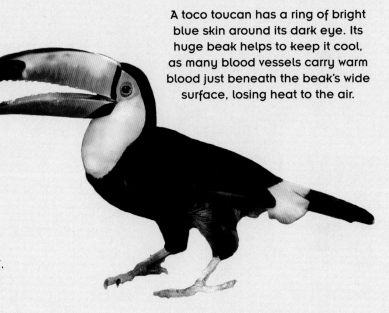

A toco toucan has a ring of bright blue skin around its dark eye. Its huge beak helps to keep it cool, as many blood vessels carry warm blood just beneath the beak's wide surface, losing heat to the air.

Family:	Ramphastidae
Range:	The Americas, from Mexico to Argentina
Habitat:	Forest and woodland
Diet:	Fruit, plus insects, lizards, small birds, and eggs
Size:	29–65 cm (11–26 in) long

Lettered aracari   Toco toucan

BIRDS OF PREY

Birds of prey eat animals—from mice and snakes to antelope—that are large in comparison with their own size. These hunters have curved beaks and sharp hooked claws, called talons, for grasping and killing prey.

The secretarybird runs after lizards, snakes, and hares with its wings spread, helping to distract its prey before it attacks.

Secretarybird

Despite their similar claws and beaks, birds of prey are in several different groups, which are not all closely related to each other. They include owls, which usually hunt at night; large and powerful eagles; swift-flying falcons; agile hawks; and vultures, which feed mostly on animals that are already dead, called carrion. While most birds of prey hunt on the wing—by mid-air chases or sudden swoops—the secretarybird hunts on the ground, by stamping on its prey.

Red-tailed hawk

When diving through the air after smaller birds, the peregrine falcon reaches a speed of 389 km per hour (242 mph), making it the world's fastest animal.

Peregrine falcon

The red-tailed hawk swoops on squirrels and mice, seizing them with its talons.

The most widespread bird of prey, the peregrine falcon can even be found in cities, where it nests on tall buildings.

The bald eagle's eyes are four times more powerful than a human's, enabling it to spot a moving rabbit around 0.5 km (0.3 miles) away as it flies.

Bald eagle

Birds of prey have larger eyes than other birds, helping them to spot distant prey. While most birds have eyes on the sides of their head, to see approaching predators, birds of prey have forward-facing eyes. This means the two eyes work together to judge the distance and speed of prey. Many birds of prey, particularly night-hunting owls, have excellent hearing. An owl can turn its head through 280 degrees, helping it to pinpoint where a sound is coming from. While most birds of prey have a poor sense of smell, a turkey vulture can smell a dead animal over half a mile away.

Its ears are positioned at different heights, so a sound reaches them at slightly different times, helping the bird judge distance and position.

Snowy owl

White plumage helps this owl to go unnoticed on the snow and ice of the Arctic.

FLAMINGOS

The long legs of a flamingo are suited to wading in shallow water, where it feeds on shrimp and algae. The flamingo's pink or red plumage is gained from pigments in these creatures. The healthier the flamingo, the brighter its feathers and the more likely it is to find a mate.

A flamingo uses its long neck to reach down to the lakebed or seabed. Its strong hooked beak stirs up the mud, which it does with its head upside down, so mud and water are cupped in the upper beak. The beak is lined with comblike plates, which trap small creatures inside the mouth as the water runs out.

When it is time to mate, large numbers of flamingos gather in areas where there is plenty of food. Groups of flamingos perform long dances to attract a mate. They walk up and down together, bending their necks, turning their heads, bowing, or flashing their wings.

After mating, a female flamingo lays a single egg on a mound of mud.

About two weeks after hatching, chicks may join crèches, groups of up to 300,000 chicks that are watched over by a small number of adults. This gives the parents more time to find food for themselves and their chicks. By staying in a crowd, the chicks have some safety from predators.

A greater flamingo's feathers are made pink by the same pigments that are found in carrots.

Family:	Phoenicopteridae
Range:	Tropical and subtropical Africa, Europe, Asia, and the Americas
Habitat:	Lakes and ocean coasts
Diet:	Shrimp, algae, small fish, and insects
Size:	1–1.5 m (3.3–4.9 ft) long

Lesser flamingo   Greater flamingo

Male lesser flamingos perform a courtship dance in Lake Nakuru, in Kenya.

PARROTS

There are around 400 species of parrots, in three groups: "true" parrots, cockatoos, and New Zealand parrots. The true parrot group includes conures, macaws, and parakeets. Parrots have a strong, curved beak, which most use for cracking nuts and seeds.

In the wild, this bird lives for 30 to 35 years.

A macaw's face has a patch that is almost bare of feathers.

Blue-and-yellow macaw

The large upper beak can move freely due to a hinged joint, enabling it to bite down hard on nuts.

It uses its long beak to rip bark from trees in search of sweet sap and insects to lick up with its tongue.

The bright plumage blends in among the green leaves, blue shadows, flowers, and fruit of the rain forest.

New Zealand kaka

It has clawed zygodactyl feet, with two toes facing forward and two back, which are useful for climbing trees and holding food.

A member of the New Zealand parrot group, the kaka lives in the forests of New Zealand.

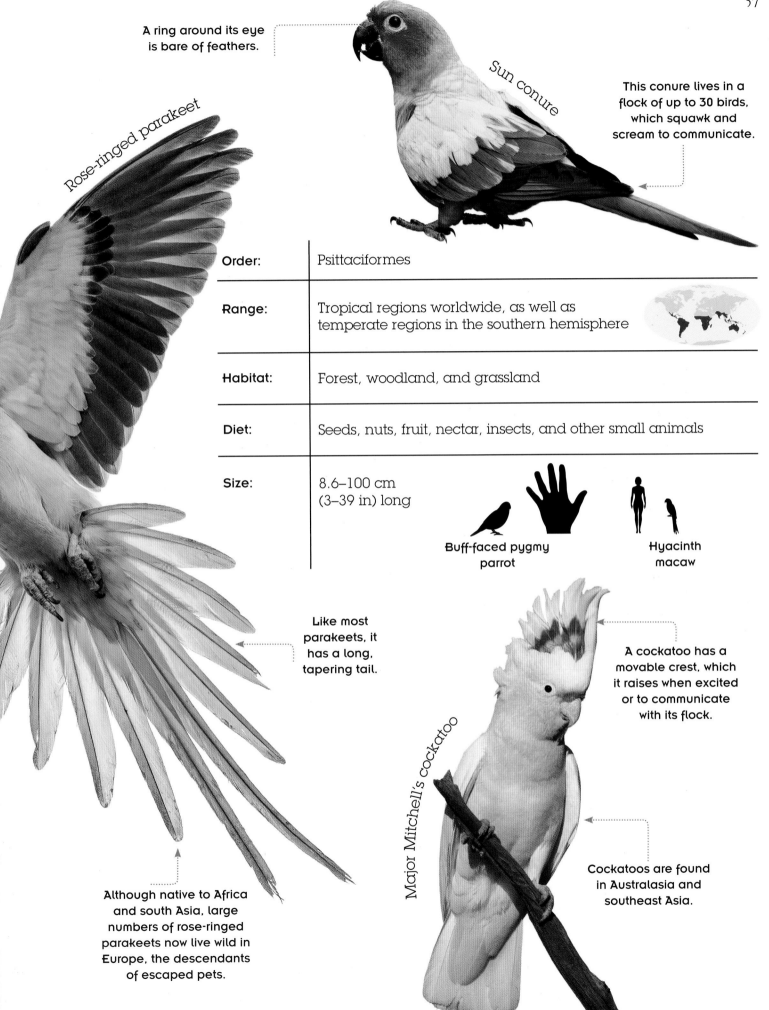

A ring around its eye is bare of feathers.

Rose-ringed parakeet

Sun conure

This conure lives in a flock of up to 30 birds, which squawk and scream to communicate.

Order:	Psittaciformes
Range:	Tropical regions worldwide, as well as temperate regions in the southern hemisphere
Habitat:	Forest, woodland, and grassland
Diet:	Seeds, nuts, fruit, nectar, insects, and other small animals
Size:	8.6–100 cm (3–39 in) long

Buff-faced pygmy parrot

Hyacinth macaw

Like most parakeets, it has a long, tapering tail.

Although native to Africa and south Asia, large numbers of rose-ringed parakeets now live wild in Europe, the descendants of escaped pets.

Major Mitchell's cockatoo

A cockatoo has a movable crest, which it raises when excited or to communicate with its flock.

Cockatoos are found in Australasia and southeast Asia.

A female pileated woodpecker has brought food for her chicks, which are safe in a nest excavated by the male.

WOODPECKERS

Woodpeckers have strong beaks, which they use for drilling nest holes in trees, as well as for drumming to communicate. They feed on insects and spiders that live on or under bark, which they extract with their beak and long, sticky tongue.

Much of a woodpecker's time is spent drilling trees with its sharp beak, by pecking up to 20 times per second. This repeated impact would cause brain damage if the bird's skull did not have sponge-like bone around the forehead and back regions, which absorb some of the blows. Even so, the woodpecker's skull heats up during drilling, which is why the bird takes frequent breaks to cool down. During drilling, a see-through eyelid closes, to protect the eye from flying wood.

Like most birds, woodpeckers make calls to communicate with each other: to warn of danger, attract a mate, or keep other birds out of their territory. Calls include whistles, wails, rattles, and high-pitched notes. To keep rivals away, woodpeckers—particularly males—also drum with their beak on hollow trees or humanmade objects such as pipes. Each species has its own pattern of drumming, with an exact number of beats and rhythm.

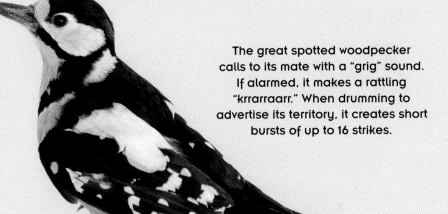

The great spotted woodpecker calls to its mate with a "grig" sound. If alarmed, it makes a rattling "krrarraarr." When drumming to advertise its territory, it creates short bursts of up to 16 strikes.

Family:	Picidae
Range:	Africa, Europe, Asia, and the Americas
Habitat:	Usually forest or woodland, but occasionally rocky or desert areas
Diet:	Insects, spiders, fruit, nuts, and tree sap
Size:	7–58 cm (3–23 in) long

Bar-breasted piculet

Great slaty woodpecker

FLIGHTLESS BIRDS

Around 60 species of birds cannot fly. All living flightless birds have wings, although they are usually smaller and weaker than those of other birds. Flightless birds may use their wings as paddles in water, for balance while running, or during displays to attract a mate.

About half of flightless birds are waterbirds, such as penguins (see page 64), which have evolved to be good swimmers instead of flyers. Others flightless birds live on islands where there are no large predators, reducing the need for flight. The islands of New Zealand have more flightless birds than any other region: 16. Until humans arrived around the year 1300, the only large predators in New Zealand were bigger birds. Humans have driven many island-dwelling flightless birds to extinction, including New Zealand's moas and Mauritius's dodo.

North Island brown kiwi

The kiwi's beak is used for plucking insects and worms from soil.

The ostrich feeds on seeds, fruit, flowers, and insects in Africa.

Around 40 cm (16 in) tall, this kiwi lives on New Zealand's North Island. It is a ratite, related to ostriches and emus.

Common ostrich

Darwin's rhea

This one-week-old chick will take three years to grow to its full height of 1 m (3.3 ft).

Found in northern Australia, Indonesia, and Papua New Guinea, this cassowary has a horny ridge known as a casque.

Southern cassowary

In a group of flightless birds known as ratites, eight species—the emu, two ostriches, two rheas, and three cassowaries—have evolved to be extremely large, which gives them some protection from predators. The largest bird of all is the common ostrich, which can grow to 2.8 m (9.2 ft) tall. To further help them escape predators, large ratites are excellent runners, with the common ostrich reaching 70 km per hour (43 mph). These birds also have sharp claws, which can deliver a deadly blow even to large predators.

The middle one of its three toes has a dagger-like claw 12.5 cm (5 in) long.

The emu swallows small stones to help grind up tough plants in its stomach.

Emu

The small wings are entirely hidden by feathers.

When running, the emu's long, featherless legs can take strides of up to 2.75 m (9 ft).

Like other ratites, Australia's emu has soft, hairlike feathers.

PEAFOWL

There are three species of peafowl, the Indian peafowl and green peafowl, from Asia, and the Congo peafowl, from Africa. Male peafowl are called peacocks, while females are peahens. Peacocks of the Asian species have extremely long tail feathers with eyespots.

Indian and green peacocks have bright plumage that is iridescent, so it appears to change shade when seen from different angles. They have long tail coverts, which are feathers that cover the base of the upper tail feathers. Most of these covert feathers have an eye-like pattern at their tip, called eyespots. When trying to attract a female, a male fans out his covert feathers and quivers them so they catch the light. Although the Congo peacock's plumage is less impressive than his Asian relatives, he also fans his shorter tail feathers to attract a mate. In addition, peacocks often make loud, high-pitched calls at mating time.

Peahens of all species are smaller and have shorter tail feathers than males. In particular, the Indian peahen looks much duller than her mate.

She has largely brown plumage with only an iridescent green neck, while the male is bright blue and green. In all species, it is the female who chooses a mate, not the male. Scientists have noticed that Indian and green peahens prefer males with many eyespots, probably because healthy tail feathers are a sign of a healthy bird.

The covert feathers of an Indian peacock grow up to 1.7 m (5.6 ft) long. This peacock is native to India and Sri Lanka, but today can be found in parks and gardens worldwide.

Family:	Phasianidae
Range:	Central Africa and southern Asia
Habitat:	Forest, grassland, and farmland
Diet:	Fruit, seeds, insects, spiders, worms, and small reptiles
Size:	0.6–3 m (2–9.8 ft) long

Congo peafowl   Green peafowl

Like all peafowl, the green peafowl has a crest of feathers on its head. Its neck and breast feathers are green and scalelike.

PENGUINS

Penguins are seabirds with wings so suited to swimming that they cannot fly. The 18 penguin species live in the southern hemisphere, apart from the Galápagos penguin, which nests on islands around the equator. Adélie, chinstrap, emperor, gentoo, and macaroni penguins are found in Antarctica.

Its white front and black back mean a predator in the water below has difficulty seeing the penguin against the sunlight, but from above the penguin appears dark against the depths.

Air is trapped in the plumage, keeping the penguin warm and helping it float.

Although they spend three-quarters of their life at sea, emperor penguins raise their chicks on Antarctica.

The wings are shaped like flippers, suited to pulling through water but too small for flying.

Chinstrap penguin

Emperor penguin adult and chicks

The feet are webbed (with toes joined by skin) to help with paddling through water.

When a chick is around 50 days old, it joins a crèche with thousands of others, looked after by a small number of adults.

Long yellow and black feathers form a crest.

Its strong beak and spiny tongue are used for grabbing slippery fish.

Southern rockhopper penguin

Humboldt penguin

Gentoo penguin

Unlike most penguins, which slide on their bellies or waddle on land, the rockhopper jumps over rocks and other obstacles.

The fastest-swimming bird, the gentoo reaches 36 km per hour (22 mph) while diving for krill.

Family:	Spheniscidae
Range:	Antarctica, southern Africa, Australasia, and South America
Habitat:	Ocean, remote coasts, and islands
Diet:	Krill, squid, and fish
Size:	30–120 cm (12–47 in) long

Little penguin

Emperor penguin

Chapter 4

Amphibians

Amphibian means "both lives" in ancient Greek, as most amphibians spend part of their life in water and part on land. A typical amphibian starts life in freshwater, taking oxygen from the water using body parts called gills. As it grows, an amphibian usually loses its gills and grows lungs for breathing air.

There are around 8,000 species of amphibians. Nearly 90 percent are anurans: the frogs and toads. These amphibians have four legs and webbed clawless toes. They start life as swimming, gilled larvae. As adults, they have lungs. Although most live around freshwater or in damp habitats, such as rain forests, some have evolved to survive in deserts. In dry habitats, most anurans spend much of their time buried in the damp soil or are active only during the cooler nights.

The second largest group of amphibians is the salamanders. These have a slender body and long tail. Some have four legs, while others have two. As adults, some have lungs for breathing air, some have gills for taking oxygen from water, and a few breathe only through their skin (see "Amphibian Skin").

The smallest group of amphibians, with only around 200 species, is the caecilians. These wormlike amphibians have no arms or legs. They spend most of their life burrowing underground in the world's warmer regions. The largest grow up to 1.5 m (4.9 ft) long.

This Asiatic tailed caecilian lays eggs in wet soil. After hatching, the larvae seek out streams.

Amphibian Skin

Amphibians usually have thin, scale-less skin. As long as the skin remains damp, oxygen can pass through it. This means that a gill-less adult amphibian can still get the oxygen it needs from the oxygen contained in water. Amphibians have glands that make thick mucus to keep their skin damp. Many amphibians also have glands that make a poisonous or bad-tasting substance.

Like the oriental fire-bellied toad, many amphibians use brightly patterned skin to advertise that they are deadly or disgusting to eat. Called aposematism, this warning deters most predators from attacking.

Like many amphibians, the splendid leaf frog is nocturnal so it does not dry out during the heat of day. At night, it hunts for insects, slugs, and worms in the rain forest.

METAMORPHOSIS

Most amphibians go through metamorphosis, which means "transformation" in ancient Greek. A typical amphibian lays eggs in freshwater. The eggs hatch into water-living larvae with gills. The larvae later transform into water- or land-living adults.

Most frogs, toads, and salamanders lay a large number of eggs, usually a few hundred, although the number ranges from just 1 to 25,000. Only around 1 in 50 of the eggs will hatch. The others may dry out or be eaten by predators. An egg is surrounded by a jelly-like protective coating. After hatching, amphibians usually spend a few weeks or months as larvae before undergoing metamorphosis. Most caecilians and a few frogs and salamanders give birth to live young that already look like small adults and do not go through metamorphosis.

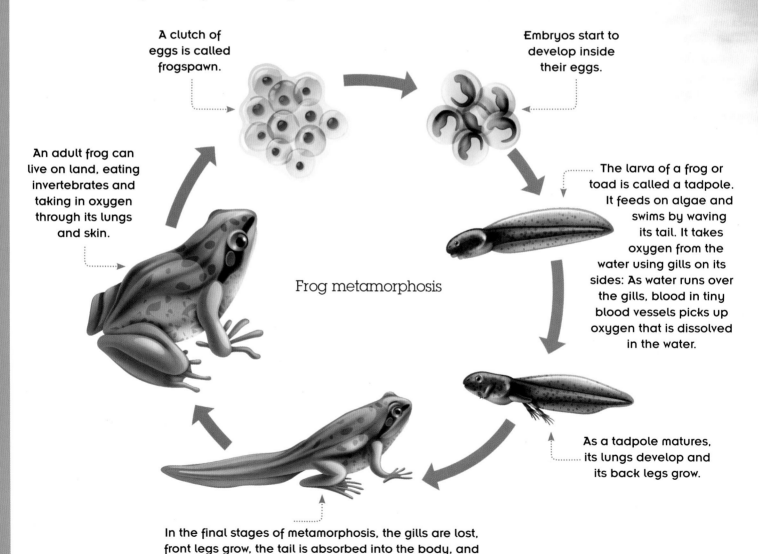

A clutch of eggs is called frogspawn.

Embryos start to develop inside their eggs.

An adult frog can live on land, eating invertebrates and taking in oxygen through its lungs and skin.

Frog metamorphosis

The larva of a frog or toad is called a tadpole. It feeds on algae and swims by waving its tail. It takes oxygen from the water using gills on its sides: As water runs over the gills, blood in tiny blood vessels picks up oxygen that is dissolved in the water.

As a tadpole matures, its lungs develop and its back legs grow.

In the final stages of metamorphosis, the gills are lost, front legs grow, the tail is absorbed into the body, and the mouth widens for the change to a meat-eating diet.

As an adult, the common frog lives near a pond or marsh, but it returns to the water to lay eggs.

Frogspawn

Some amphibians do not lay their eggs in freshwater but in damp soil or wet leaves. The smoky jungle frog makes a hollow in the ground for its eggs, which hatch when the hollow is flooded. The red-eyed tree frog lays eggs on a leaf above a pool. When the tadpoles hatch, they slip into the water. Around one in five amphibians shows some care for its eggs or tadpoles, bringing water to keep the eggs moist or carrying the tadpoles to water after hatching. The male common midwife toad carries the female's eggs on his hind legs, soaking them in a pond whenever they get too dry.

This frog is carrying its tadpoles to a pool, where they will live as they develop into adults.

A female sky-blue poison frog lays her eggs under damp leaves on the floor of the rain forest.

Sky-blue poison frog

FROGS

These tailless amphibians often have long back legs suited to jumping. Their large, protruding eyes are on either side of their head, enabling them to see all around. There are around 7,300 species of frogs. Those with wartier skin and shorter back legs are usually called toads.

Since this toad has no teeth, insects, spiders, and slugs are gulped down whole.

Its skin is covered by wartlike bumps, which are groups of poison-making glands.

Common toad

As an adult, it spends most of its time in forests, walking slowly on its four legs.

To camouflage itself in green rain forest trees, the frog shuts its eyes, covers its blue sides with its legs, and tucks its bright feet beneath its belly.

Red-eyed tree frog

This frog tries to startle predators by suddenly opening its large red eyes.

Glands in the skin make slippery mucus that makes the frog harder for predators to grip.

Long, strong back legs are suited to jumping between branches.

Sonoran desert toad

The long toes have sticky pads that help with climbing.

Just 1.5 cm (0.6 in) long, this frog lives in the Amazon rain forest.

Glands in the skin produce a poison made by eating poisonous insects.

This frog advertises its poisonousness with its bright stripes.

These leaflike "horns" help camouflage the frog on the forest floor.

Uakari poison dart frog

Argentine horned frog

It sits and waits for prey as large as mice, which it stuffs into its wide mouth using its sticky tongue.

Its legs are shorter than those of most frogs, making it a poor jumper.

These bumps, called parotoid glands, produce poison that makes the toad taste foul to predators.

Order:	Anura
Range:	Worldwide except polar regions, remote islands, and some deserts
Habitat:	Deserts to rain forests
Diet:	Usually insects and worms, but larger species eat small frogs, mice, and snakes
Size:	7.7 mm–32 cm (0.3–12.6 in) long

Paedophryne amauensis

Goliath frog

The axolotl, which has six pink and feathery
external gills, spends its whole life in water.

SALAMANDERS

There are around 650 species of salamanders. These amphibians have the amazing ability to regrow a lost leg or tail. Salamanders are born in water or in a damp, hidden spot. Some stay in water throughout their life, while others spend most of their adult life on land.

Since salamanders are thin-skinned and slow-moving, they have developed other features to keep them safe from predators. Their skin is covered by slippery mucus, which makes them difficult to grasp. Many species also make a powerful poison that makes them deadly to eat or taste horrible. These salamanders usually have bright yellow, orange, or red markings. This warns predators that they are not good to eat.

During an attack, some salamanders shed their tail. This continues to wiggle for several minutes, distracting the attacker while the salamander makes its escape. The tail regrows within a few weeks.

Around half of salamander species are at risk of extinction because of rising temperatures and the loss of their damp or watery habitats. One of the most critically endangered is the axolotl, which is now found only in one Mexican lake, where it is threatened by water pollution. Unlike most salamanders, the axolotl does not go through metamorphosis. Rather than developing lungs as it reaches adulthood, it remains in water throughout its life, absorbing oxygen from the water through its gills.

Found among damp leaves in European forests, the poisonous fire salamander catches insects and spiders with its sticky tongue.

Order:	Urodela
Range:	Temperate North America, Europe, Asia, and Africa, plus parts of tropical South America and Asia
Diet:	Small animals
Habitat:	In water, near water, or among moist plants
Size:	1.5 cm–1.8 m (0.6 in–5.9 ft) long

Arboreal minute salamander

Chinese giant salamander

Chapter 5

REPTILES

Reptiles have four legs or are descended from four-legged ancestors but have evolved to be legless. Unlike amphibians, reptiles have watertight skin covered with scales or bony plates called scutes. All reptiles have lungs for breathing air and most lay eggs on land.

There are four surviving orders of reptiles: squamates, turtles, crocodiles, and the tuatara. Since birds are descended from extinct reptiles called dinosaurs, they are sometimes considered to be reptiles, too. The closest living relatives of crocodiles are birds.

There are around 11,500 reptile species. The largest order is the squamates, with over 11,100 species. This group includes snakes, lizards, and amphisbaenians. These reptiles have flexible jaws that, particularly for snakes, enable them to open their mouth wide to swallow prey. Like the tuatara, the only species in its order, squamates have overlapping scales. The second largest order is the turtles. There are around 360 species of turtles, which are the only vertebrates with a complete shell. The 26 species of crocodiles have thick skin protected by scutes.

Reptiles are ectothermic, which means they cannot raise their own body temperature but rely on being warmed by the sun. For this reason, reptiles are most common in the world's hot and warm regions. Many reptile species maintain their temperature at a healthy level by moving between the shade, to cool down, and basking in sunlight, to warm up.

There are around 200 species of amphisbaenians, including the four-toed worm lizard. Amphisbaenians are wormlike reptiles with scales arranged in rings.

Found only in New Zealand, the tuatara has a spiny crest on its back, two rows of teeth in its upper jaw, and no earholes.

Reptile Eggs

Reptiles evolved from amphibians around 312 million years ago. Unlike amphibians, they lay eggs with a tough shell, which stops the growing baby drying out on land. This development let reptiles move away from water and colonize the land. However, a few lizards and around 20 percent of snakes later evolved to give birth to live young.

A corn snake hatches from its egg. All egg-laying reptiles, even those that live in water, lay their eggs on land.

SNAKES

These long-bodied, limbless reptiles are meat-eaters. Of almost 4,000 snake species, about 600 make venom that stuns or kills prey. These snakes inject their venom using long, pointed teeth called fangs. Other snakes eat their prey while it is still alive or kill it by constriction.

To scare away predators, this non-venomous snake evolved to look like the venomous coral snake.

Milksnake

The king cobra kills other snakes with a venomous bite, then opens its flexible jaws wide to swallow them whole.

King cobra

It frightens away predators by spreading its neck flap, raising its head, and hissing.

The longest venomous snake, it reaches 5.85 m (19.2 ft) long.

Bush viper

Venom is made in glands behind the eyes.

It injects deadly venom using hollow fangs, which fold against the roof of the mouth when not in use.

It holds prey, such as lizards, until the venom has taken effect, then swallows them whole.

Suborder:	Serpentes
Range:	Land snakes worldwide except Antarctica and islands including Iceland, Ireland, and New Zealand; sea snakes in the Indian and Pacific Oceans
Habitat:	Desert to ocean
Diet:	Animals from insects and mice to other snakes and antelope
Size:	10 cm–6.95 m (4 in–22.8 ft) long

Barbados threadsnake

Reticulated python

This snake moves by waving its body, gripping the ground with the wider scales on its belly, and pushing against rocks.

This South American boa coils tightly around prey until the victim's blood stops flowing.

Boa constrictor

Western diamondback rattlesnake

To warn away predators, it shakes interlocking horny segments in its tail, making a rattling noise.

Like all snakes, it uses its forked tongue to smell and taste particles in the air to detect prey.

A male panther chameleon can change its skin shade, becoming brighter as a sign of aggression and darker when it submits to a rival.

LIZARDS

Most lizards have a long tail and four legs, although some are legless. A few lizards grow to a great size, but they are usually small animals. The majority are meat-eaters, often sitting and waiting for prey, then snatching it with their long tongue or jaws.

Legged lizards must bend their body from side to side as they run, first on their left back leg and then their right. This squeezes their lungs and prevents them running far. Lizards have other strategies to escape predators. Small lizards, such as Aegean wall lizards, dart for the nearest hole or crack. Most lizards are camouflaged by skin that is shaded and patterned to blend in with their environment. A few, including the Moorish gecko, can slowly change their skin shade to match their surroundings.

When cornered, horned lizards squirt foul-tasting blood from a pouch beneath their eyes. Many lizard species, including geckos, will shed their tail if it is caught. The tail continues to wriggle to distract the predator, while the gecko makes its escape and then regrows a new tail over several weeks.

Lizards often signal to each other to attract a mate or drive others away from their territory. Physical signals include tail-wagging, mouth-opening, and tongue-flashing. Some lizards display bright body parts, such as neck flaps called dewlaps.

When threatened by a predator, the frilled lizard extends its neck frill to appear larger and more frightening.

Suborder:	Lacertilia
Range:	Worldwide except polar regions and some islands 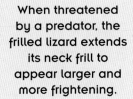
Habitat:	Desert to forest, usually on the ground but sometimes in trees, underground, or in coastal waters
Diet:	Usually small invertebrates but larger species eat fish, birds, and mammals, while some iguanas are plant-eaters
Size:	2 cm–3.1 m (0.8 in–10.3 ft) long

Jaragua dwarf gecko

Komodo dragon

SCALES AND SCUTES

Reptile skin is protected by scales or scutes, which contain keratin, the same strong material found in hair, nails, and feathers. This tough covering prevents reptiles from drying out, protects them from predators, and helps with gripping as they crawl or slither.

Scales are small, hard plates of keratin. They form in the outer layer of skin. Lizards have overlapping scales that may be shaped into spines for display or protection. Snakes have overlapping scales of different shapes and sizes, as well as scutes on their belly. Scutes are bony plates formed in a deeper layer of skin, covered by an outer layer of keratin. Crocodiles and turtles have scutes. A turtle's shell usually has 54 large scutes.

Males have larger cone-shaped scales on their head.

A row of spine-shaped scales helps to soak up sunlight.

Marine iguana

The only sea-dwelling lizard, the marine iguana is covered by small, overlapping scales.

The skin of the head has no scales or scutes but is covered by a layer of keratin.

A member of the crocodile order, this well-protected caiman has rows of thick, ridged scutes on its back.

Scutes on the tail are triangular and sharp.

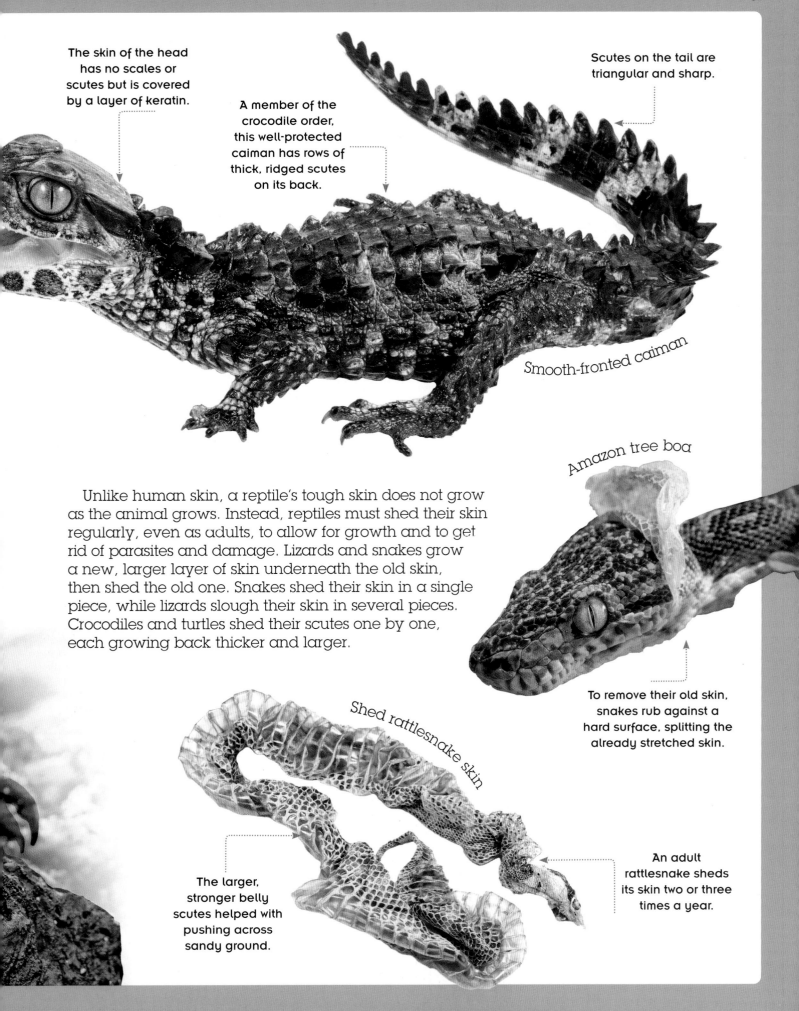

Smooth-fronted caiman

Amazon tree boa

Unlike human skin, a reptile's tough skin does not grow as the animal grows. Instead, reptiles must shed their skin regularly, even as adults, to allow for growth and to get rid of parasites and damage. Lizards and snakes grow a new, larger layer of skin underneath the old skin, then shed the old one. Snakes shed their skin in a single piece, while lizards slough their skin in several pieces. Crocodiles and turtles shed their scutes one by one, each growing back thicker and larger.

To remove their old skin, snakes rub against a hard surface, splitting the already stretched skin.

Shed rattlesnake skin

The larger, stronger belly scutes helped with pushing across sandy ground.

An adult rattlesnake sheds its skin two or three times a year.

CROCODILES

The crocodile order contains 26 species of true crocodiles, alligators, caimans, and gharials. These large meat-eating reptiles are semiaquatic, spending part of their life in water and part on land. They have long snouts, four legs, and powerful tails for swimming.

All 26 crocodile species have a similar body shape. However, gharials have a narrower snout than their relatives. A true crocodile has upper and lower jaws of the same width, so both its upper and lower teeth are visible when the mouth is closed. In contrast, alligators and caimans have small hollows in the upper jaw into which their lower teeth fit. Caimans are smaller than alligators and have tougher skin.

Most of these reptiles catch prey by stalking then ambushing. Their eyes, nostrils, and ears are on the top of the head, so they can remain largely hidden beneath the water as they watch and follow. At the last moment, they rush to snatch prey in their jaws.

Different species have differently shaped teeth and snouts to suit their particular prey. With its sharp teeth and slender snout, the Indian gharial catches slippery fish. The blunt-toothed Chinese alligator crushes shellfish. None of these reptiles can chew their food, so small prey is swallowed whole and larger prey is ripped to pieces by pulling with the jaws or left until it rots.

Weighing up to 453 kg (999 lb), the American alligator reaches a speed of 16 km per hour (10 mph) on land and 32 km per hour (20 mph) in water.

Order:	Crocodilia
Range:	Tropical regions worldwide, as well as the southeastern United States, southern Africa, and eastern China
Habitat:	In and around swamps, rivers, lakes, and coastal oceans
Diet:	Animals from insects, frogs, and shellfish to birds, mammals, and other reptiles
Size:	1.2–6.8 m (3.9–22.3 ft) long

Cuvier's dwarf caiman

Saltwater crocodile

An American crocodile lies in wait in a coastal seagrass bed. True crocodiles are more aggressive than other members of the order.

TURTLES

To protect them from predators, turtles have a shell, which is formed partly from extended, joined rib bones. The shell's upper part, called the carapace, is dome-shaped, while the flatter underside is called the plastron. Turtles live on land, in freshwater, or in the ocean.

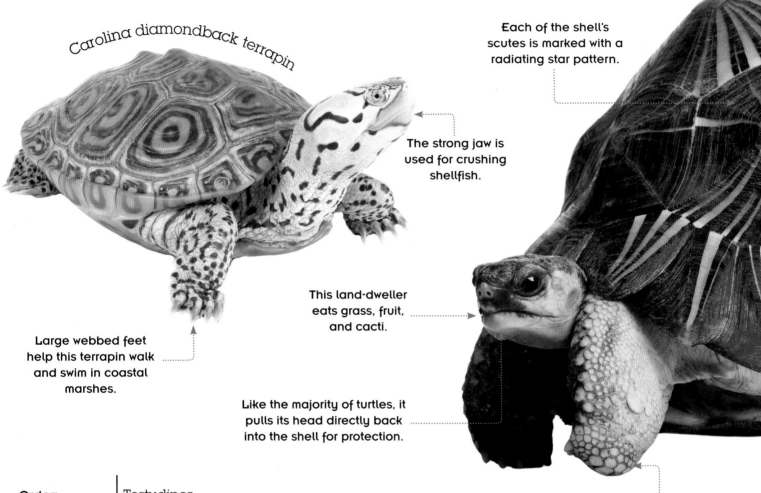

Carolina diamondback terrapin

Each of the shell's scutes is marked with a radiating star pattern.

The strong jaw is used for crushing shellfish.

This land-dweller eats grass, fruit, and cacti.

Large webbed feet help this terrapin walk and swim in coastal marshes.

Like the majority of turtles, it pulls its head directly back into the shell for protection.

It crawls slowly across shrubland with an average speed of 0.2–0.5 km per hour (0.1–0.3 mph).

It lives in South American rivers and lakes.

Order:	Testudines
Range:	Tropical, subtropical, and some temperate regions
Habitat:	Desert, rain forest, ponds, rivers, and ocean
Diet:	Plants and small animals
Size:	6 cm–2.2 m (2.4 in–7.2 ft) long

Speckled tortoise   Leatherback sea turtle

This turtle's body fat turns green from its diet of sea grasses and algae.

Green sea turtle

Radiated tortoise

Like the other six species of sea turtles, it pulls through the water with its flipper-shaped limbs.

During the day, it warms up in the sunlight by basking on rocks.

Painted turtle

This tortoise can live for 188 years or more.

This pond-dweller rips at small water creatures with its claws.

Geoffroy's side-necked turtle

The carapace has an overhang to protect the head.

This turtle draws its head and neck sideways into its shell.

Chapter 6

FISH

Fish are water-dwelling animals that take oxygen from water using gills. They have streamlined bodies and fins, which help with swimming. Most fish have skin covered by small, hard plates called scales. Fish usually lay jelly-like eggs in the water.

There are over 34,000 species of fish, living in oceans, rivers, lakes, or wetlands. They are in three main groups: bony, cartilaginous, and jawless fish. Around 97 percent of fish are bony fish, with skeletons made of bone. Most bony fish have smooth, overlapping scales and swim bladders, which are gas-filled sacs that help them float.

The bony fish are in two subgroups: ray-finned fish and lobe-finned fish. Nearly all are ray-finned. Their fins are webs of skin supported by bony or horny spines called rays. There are just eight species of lobe-finned fish, the coelacanths and lungfish, which have fleshy fins. As with all fish, fins in different places help with moving forward, turning, and balance. Gills may be caudal (tail), dorsal (along the back), pectoral (on the sides), pelvic (on the underside near the head), or anal (on the underside near the tail).

There are around 1,000 species of cartilaginous fish, which have skeletons made of bendy cartilage. Cartilaginous fish include sharks and rays. Around 120 species of hagfish and lampreys make up the jawless fish, which feed by sucking up prey. Unlike other fish, they have no scales.

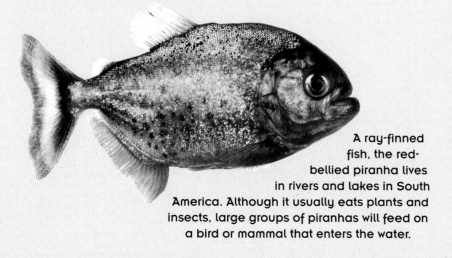

A ray-finned fish, the red-bellied piranha lives in rivers and lakes in South America. Although it usually eats plants and insects, large groups of piranhas will feed on a bird or mammal that enters the water.

Hiding in a brain coral, a secretary blenny waits for a passing invertebrate to grab.

Fish Gills

Like all animals, fish need oxygen to survive. Water contains oxygen, which fish extract using body parts called gills, which lie on both sides of the throat. Fish draw in mouthfuls of water, which flows through the gills. These are threadlike structures containing countless tiny blood vessels. The oxygen passes through the blood vessels' thin walls and into the blood.

This cutaway illustration shows a bony fish's gills. Bony fish have a single gill opening, through which water exits the gills, protected by a bony covering called the operculum.

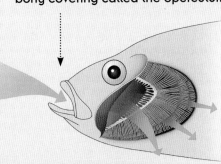

SHARKS

Sharks have skeletons made of light, bendy cartilage rather than bone. Of more than 500 species of sharks, over 70 are endangered, largely because of fishing by humans. Although most sharks are hunters, three species—including the whale shark—strain their food from the water.

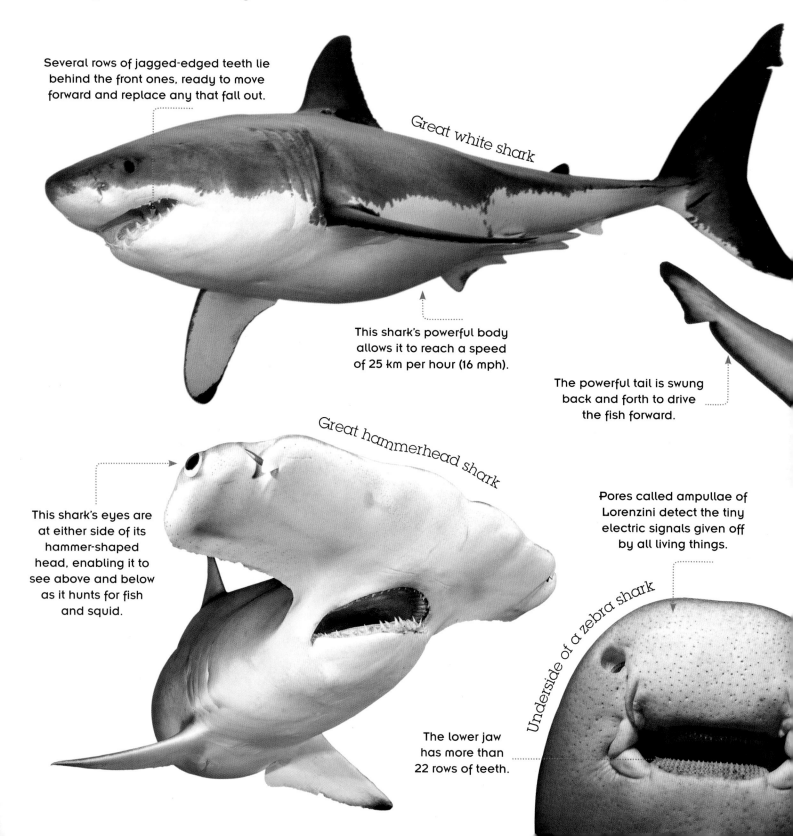

Several rows of jagged-edged teeth lie behind the front ones, ready to move forward and replace any that fall out.

Great white shark

This shark's powerful body allows it to reach a speed of 25 km per hour (16 mph).

The powerful tail is swung back and forth to drive the fish forward.

Great hammerhead shark

This shark's eyes are at either side of its hammer-shaped head, enabling it to see above and below as it hunts for fish and squid.

Pores called ampullae of Lorenzini detect the tiny electric signals given off by all living things.

Underside of a zebra shark

The lower jaw has more than 22 rows of teeth.

Superorder:	Selachimorpha
Range:	Atlantic, Indian, Pacific, and Arctic Oceans
Habitat:	Coastal ocean, open ocean to 3,000 m (9,840 ft) deep, and occasionally rivers
Diet:	Animals from tiny krill and larvae to fish, dolphins, and seals
Size:	0.2–18.8 m (8 in–62 ft) long

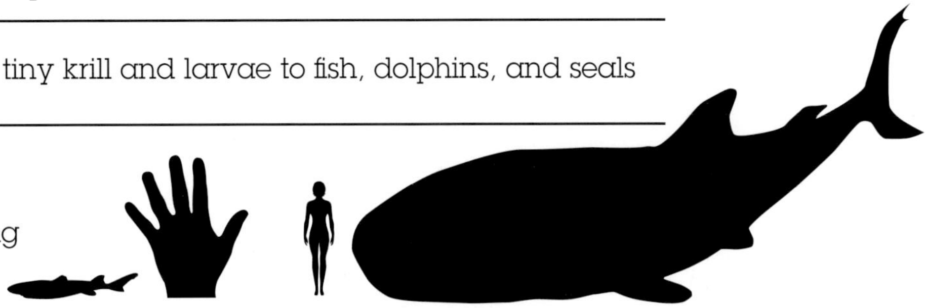

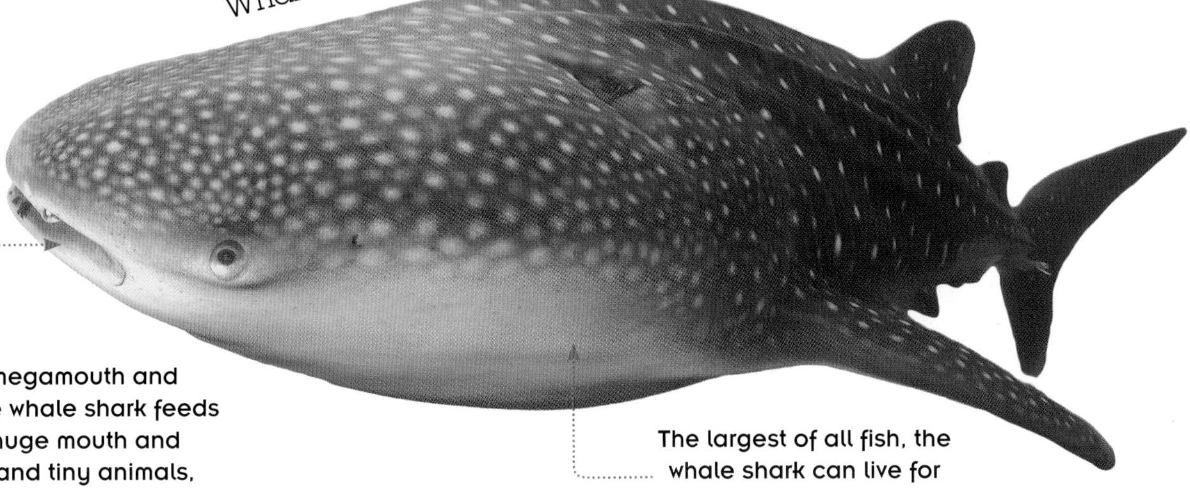

Dwarf lanternshark

Whale shark

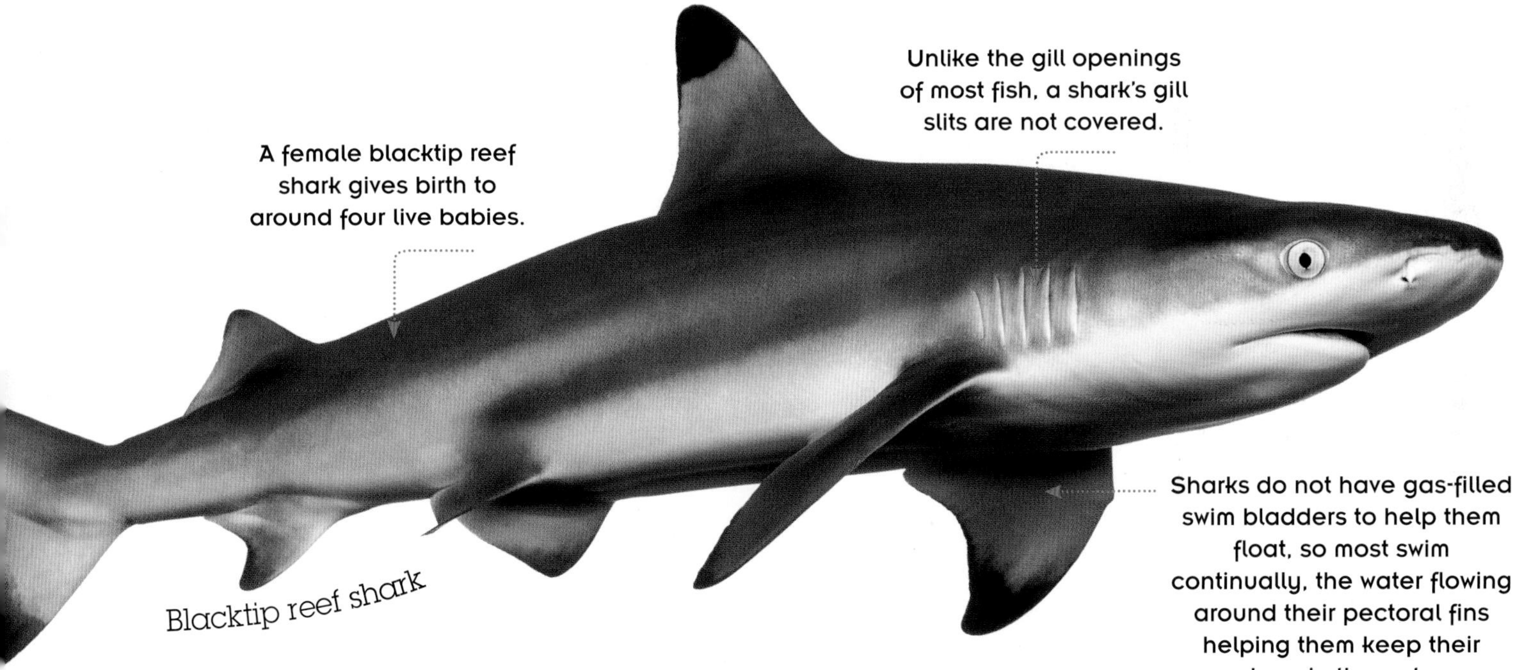

A female blacktip reef shark gives birth to around four live babies.

Unlike the gill openings of most fish, a shark's gill slits are not covered.

Blacktip reef shark

Sharks do not have gas-filled swim bladders to help them float, so most swim continually, the water flowing around their pectoral fins helping them keep their place in the water.

Whale shark

Barbels below the nostrils taste the water for traces of prey.

Along with the megamouth and basking sharks, the whale shark feeds by opening its huge mouth and sucking in water and tiny animals, which are strained out by filter pads.

The largest of all fish, the whale shark can live for up to 130 years.

Denise's pygmy seahorse is perfectly camouflaged as it waits for prey on a red and white sea fan.

SEAHORSES

Seahorses have a long, horselike snout. Their tail is prehensile, which means it can grasp objects by curling around them. Unlike most bony fish, they do not have scales but are protected by a covering of bony plates. There are around 50 species of seahorse.

Unlike most fish, seahorses swim upright rather than horizontally. Their bony plates prevent them from wiggling their body, so they move by fluttering their dorsal (back) fin. As a result, seahorses move very slowly, with the dwarf seahorse reaching just 1.5 m per hour (5 ft per hour), making it the slowest fish of all.

Seahorses do not swim after prey or to escape predators. Instead, they curl their tail around coral, seagrass, or seaweed and wait for prey to come within reach. Prey is then sucked up through the snout. Seahorses are well camouflaged as they wait, often with bumps or spikes that mimic their rocky or frondy habitat. They can also change their skin shade to match their surroundings, using skin cells called chromatophores, which contain different pigments. Moving muscles around the chromatophores results in different shades being displayed.

When seahorses mate, the female deposits her eggs in a pouch on the male's belly, where he fertilizes them. Two to four weeks later, the male gives birth, squeezing the babies out of his pouch.

This male tiger tail seahorse's pouch is swollen with up to 2,000 eggs. It is likely that only around two of the babies, called fry, will survive to adulthood.

Genus:	Hippocampus
Range:	Tropical, subtropical, and temperate Atlantic, Indian, and Pacific Oceans
Habitat:	Coastal ocean among seagrass, coral reefs, and mangroves, to a depth of 150 m (490 ft)
Diet:	Small invertebrates such as shrimp
Size:	1.4–35 cm (0.6–13.8 in) long

Satomi's pygmy seahorse

Big-belly seahorse

SCORPIONFISH

As protection from predators, scorpionfish have sharp spines which can inject venomous mucus. Most scorpionfish lie in wait for prey on the ocean floor, where they are camouflaged among coral, rocks, or algae. Lionfish, which are also members of this family, ambush their prey in open water.

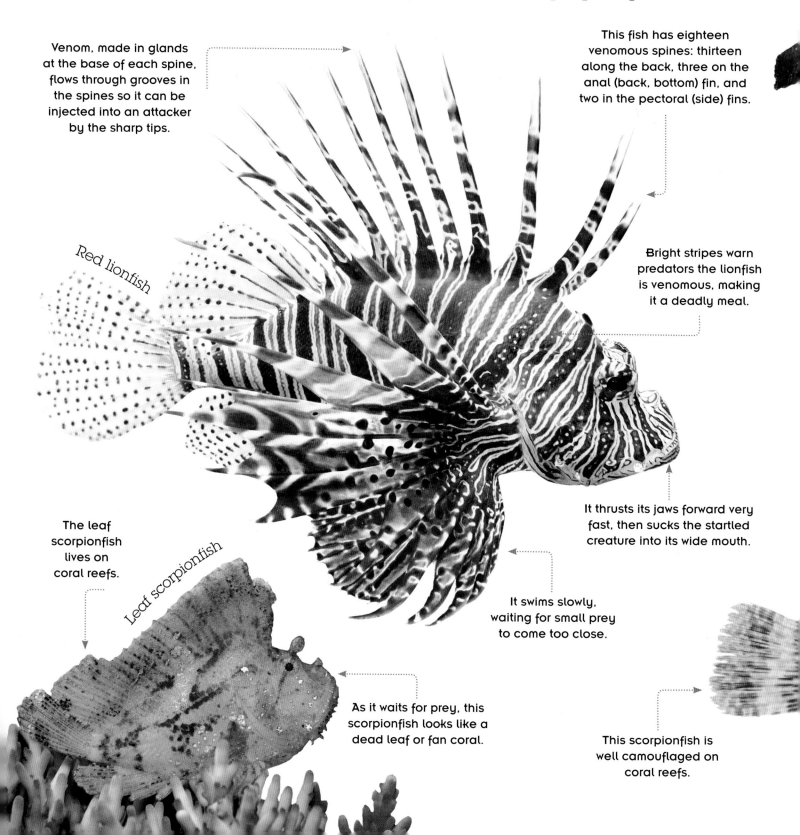

Venom, made in glands at the base of each spine, flows through grooves in the spines so it can be injected into an attacker by the sharp tips.

This fish has eighteen venomous spines: thirteen along the back, three on the anal (back, bottom) fin, and two in the pectoral (side) fins.

Red lionfish

Bright stripes warn predators the lionfish is venomous, making it a deadly meal.

The leaf scorpionfish lives on coral reefs.

Leaf scorpionfish

It thrusts its jaws forward very fast, then sucks the startled creature into its wide mouth.

It swims slowly, waiting for small prey to come too close.

As it waits for prey, this scorpionfish looks like a dead leaf or fan coral.

This scorpionfish is well camouflaged on coral reefs.

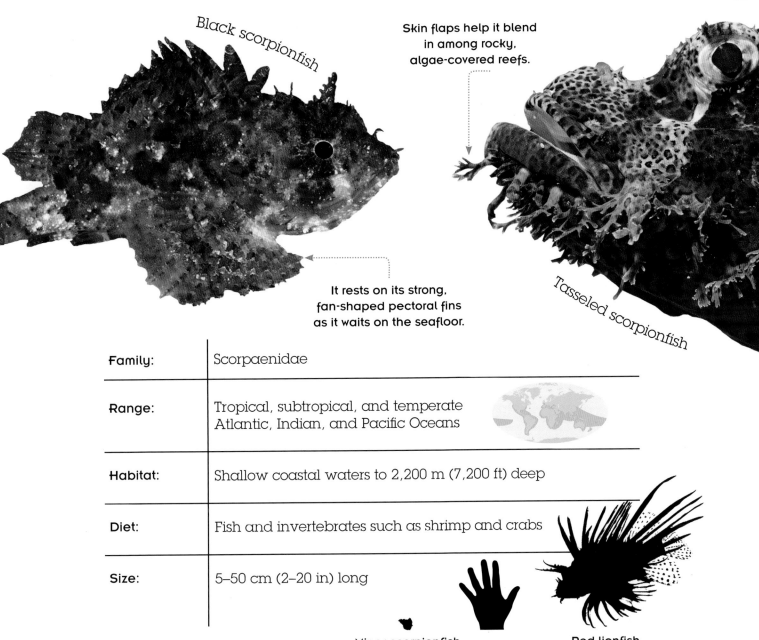

Black scorpionfish

Skin flaps help it blend in among rocky, algae-covered reefs.

It rests on its strong, fan-shaped pectoral fins as it waits on the seafloor.

Tasseled scorpionfish

Family:	Scorpaenidae
Range:	Tropical, subtropical, and temperate Atlantic, Indian, and Pacific Oceans
Habitat:	Shallow coastal waters to 2,200 m (7,200 ft) deep
Diet:	Fish and invertebrates such as shrimp and crabs
Size:	5–50 cm (2–20 in) long

Minor scorpionfish

Red lionfish

Hunchback scorpionfish

These sharp spines are charged with painful venom.

Large eyes help with night-time hunting.

It sucks in prey by opening its mouth quickly, creating empty space that the water—carrying prey with it—rushes in to fill.

CLOWNFISH

Also known as anemonefish, these small fish live among the stinging tentacles of sea anemones. The relationship between these two animals is an example of symbiosis, which means "living together" in ancient Greek.

Both clownfish and sea anemones benefit from their symbiosis. Anemones usually attach to a hard surface, catching prey with their stinging tentacles then passing it to their central mouth. Hiding among those tentacles, clownfish are safe from most predators. Clownfish are protected from anemone stings by their covering of thick mucus. Clownfish also feed on scraps left over from the anemone's meals and on dead tentacles.

In return, clownfish defend their anemone from fish that try to eat it. They also feed on parasites that attach to the anemone. Nutrients in a clownfish's excrement (poop) help the anemone grow.

All clownfish are born male, then may develop into females as they mature.

Clownfish usually live in a group, with one female, one adult male, and several young males. Only the female and adult male mate with each other. If the female dies, the adult male turns into a female to take her place.

Ocellaris clownfish can communicate with each other by making clicking and popping sounds.

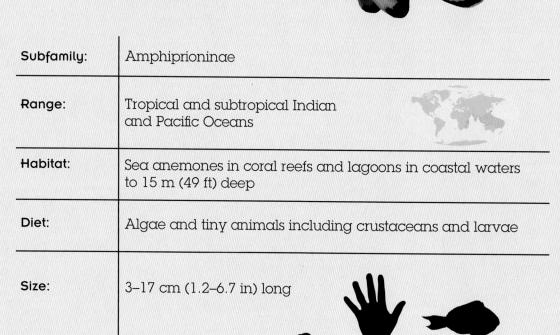

Subfamily:	Amphiprioninae
Range:	Tropical and subtropical Indian and Pacific Oceans
Habitat:	Sea anemones in coral reefs and lagoons in coastal waters to 15 m (49 ft) deep
Diet:	Algae and tiny animals including crustaceans and larvae
Size:	3–17 cm (1.2–6.7 in) long

Orange skunk clownfish

Orange fin anemonefish

A Clark's anemonefish hides in a bubble-tip anemone. Each species of clownfish lives in particular species of sea anemones.

ON A CORAL REEF

Coral reefs are found in warm, shallow water, where they provide a home for over 6,000 species of fish. Reefs offer hiding places, safe spots to lay eggs, and plenty of food, such as the corals themselves, the algae that grow on them, and the other animals attracted to the reef.

This fish's intricate pattern makes its outline hard to make out among the coral.

Many fish that live on coral reefs have vivid patterns. This helps with camouflage against the bright reef, where sunlight creates changing patterns of light and shade. Many small reef fish stay in one area of the reef, where the hiding places are known and they are well camouflaged among the particular species of coral or anemones.

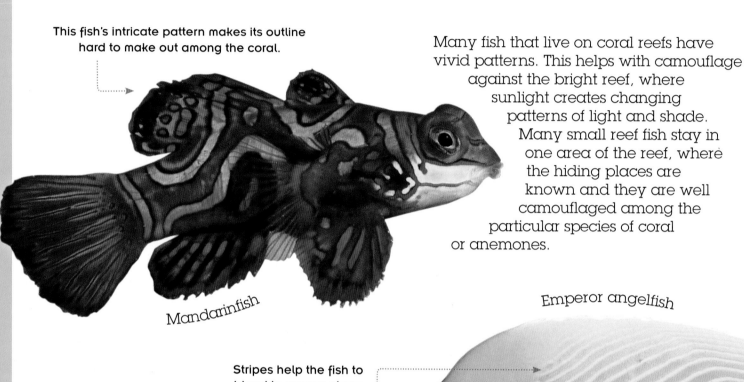

Mandarinfish

Emperor angelfish

Stripes help the fish to blend in among algae and dappled sunlight.

The anthias lives in large groups, called shoals, which offer the protection of countless eyes to watch for predators.

Lyretail anthias

The bodies of many reef fish are narrow from side to side, which enables them to hide from predators in crevices. This body shape also helps with swift changes of direction, so they can dart between corals. This contrasts with open-water fish, which have sleek, smoothly shaped bodies suited to cutting straight through the water quickly.

The tang's narrow body and long, large dorsal and anal fins help with steering left or right.

The purple tang reaches for algae growing between rocks, using its long snout.

Purple tang

Coral reefs are built by tiny invertebrates called coral polyps. The polyps, which live in colonies containing thousands of their species, build a hard skeleton around their soft body, one on top of the other. Over time, this process can build a reef, containing many different coral species, stretching for thousands of miles. Today, climate change is damaging many reefs, as polyps are sensitive to changes in water temperature.

Shoals of anthias will defend their corner of the reef from other fish.

A frightened guineafowl pufferfish has inflated itself. Its large teeth are joined together, forming a strong beak for eating tough corals.

PUFFERFISH

These fish can fill their stomach with water, inflating themselves until they are too large for most predators to swallow. In addition, some species of pufferfish are among the world's most poisonous vertebrates, containing enough poison to kill 30 adult humans.

Pufferfish are slow swimmers, moving only by waving their fins rather than by wiggling their body. They rely on strategies other than speed to escape predators. When threatened, a pufferfish quickly swallows water, inflating itself to more than double its normal size. Many species also have spines on their skin, which stand out from the body when the stomach is inflated, making the fish a spiky ball that would choke most predators if they attempted to swallow.

Many pufferfish species are highly poisonous if eaten, which deters most predators from attacking. Neurotoxins, substances that stop nerves from communicating with each other, are concentrated in their internal organs and sometimes their skin, so they can paralyze or kill a predator. A pufferfish gains its neurotoxins by consuming neurotoxin-making bacteria. Despite this, some pufferfish are considered a delicacy in parts of East Asia, where highly trained chefs serve only the body parts that are safe to eat.

This white-spotted puffer is not inflated. Its bold pattern warns predators it can be deadly to eat.

Family:	Tetraodontidae
Range:	Tropical, subtropical, and temperate Atlantic, Indian, and Pacific Oceans, plus tropical South America, Africa, and southeast Asia
Habitat:	Ocean, brackish (mixed seawater and freshwater) water, lakes, and rivers
Diet:	Algae, shellfish, and other small invertebrates
Size:	3–67 cm (1.2–26 in) long

Dwarf pufferfish   Mbu pufferfish

FLATFISH

Flatfish live on the floors of oceans and freshwater. Most fish are symmetrical, but adult flatfish have both eyes on one side of their head, enabling them to keep watch as they lie on the other side. There are around 800 different flatfish, including flounder, halibut, plaice, and sole.

Young flatfish have an eye on either side of their head. They float freely through the water. As they mature, they go through metamorphosis, during which one eye moves to the other side of the head. Afterward, the fish settles on the bottom. Different species can be recognized by usually having their eyes on either the left or right side.

Flatfish often lie on the muddy or sandy bottom with only their eyes showing. They are well camouflaged on their upper side, with speckles and shades that make them hard to spot. Some flatfish, including turbot, can match their shading to their surroundings, using skin cells called chromatophores. A flatfish's underside, or blind side, is usually white.

Some flatfish, such as flounders, eat small fish. When prey swims close, these flatfish leap off the bottom and seize it between their two toothed jaws. Most soles prey on small mud-dwelling invertebrates, such as worms, mollusks, and shrimp. These flatfish have teeth on only the lower jaw of their blind side.

The European plaice is commonly eaten by humans in northern Europe.

Order:	Pleuronectiformes
Range:	Atlantic, Indian, Pacific, Arctic, and Southern Oceans, plus South America, Africa, southeast Asia, and Australasia
Habitat:	On or near the floor of rivers, estuaries, and oceans, to over 1,500 m (4,900 ft) deep
Diet:	Fish and invertebrates such as shrimp, shellfish, and worms
Size:	8 cm–4.7 m (3 in–15.4 ft) long

Eastern Atlantic dwarf tonguefish

Atlantic halibut

A European flounder usually has its eyes on the right side of its head. The twisted shape of its mouth is a result of the movement of the skull bones.

IN THE DEEP SEA

Sunlight cannot reach more than 1,000 m (3,300 ft) below the ocean surface, leaving the deeper water dark and no warmer than around 4 °C (39 °F). No plants can survive without sunlight, so there are fewer sources of food. Deep-sea fish have many adaptations to survive the extreme conditions.

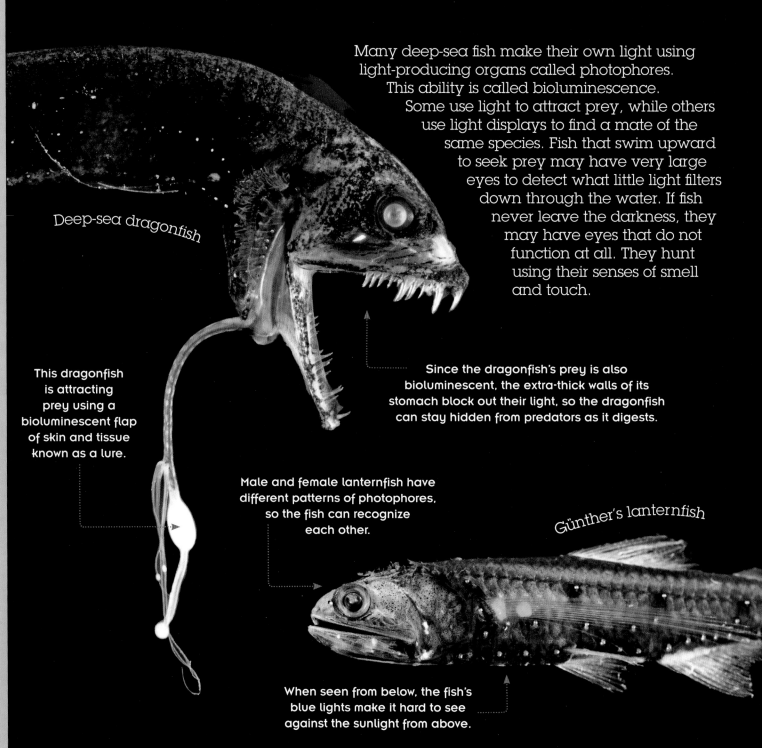

Many deep-sea fish make their own light using light-producing organs called photophores. This ability is called bioluminescence. Some use light to attract prey, while others use light displays to find a mate of the same species. Fish that swim upward to seek prey may have very large eyes to detect what little light filters down through the water. If fish never leave the darkness, they may have eyes that do not function at all. They hunt using their senses of smell and touch.

Deep-sea dragonfish

This dragonfish is attracting prey using a bioluminescent flap of skin and tissue known as a lure.

Since the dragonfish's prey is also bioluminescent, the extra-thick walls of its stomach block out their light, so the dragonfish can stay hidden from predators as it digests.

Male and female lanternfish have different patterns of photophores, so the fish can recognize each other.

Günther's lanternfish

When seen from below, the fish's blue lights make it hard to see against the sunlight from above.

Since food is scarcer in the deep ocean than in the sunlit waters above, many deep-sea fish have small bodies that need little food to sustain them. However, many have extra-large mouths and stomachs so they can swallow and digest whatever prey comes their way. Some survive on the dead animals and waste that floats down from above.

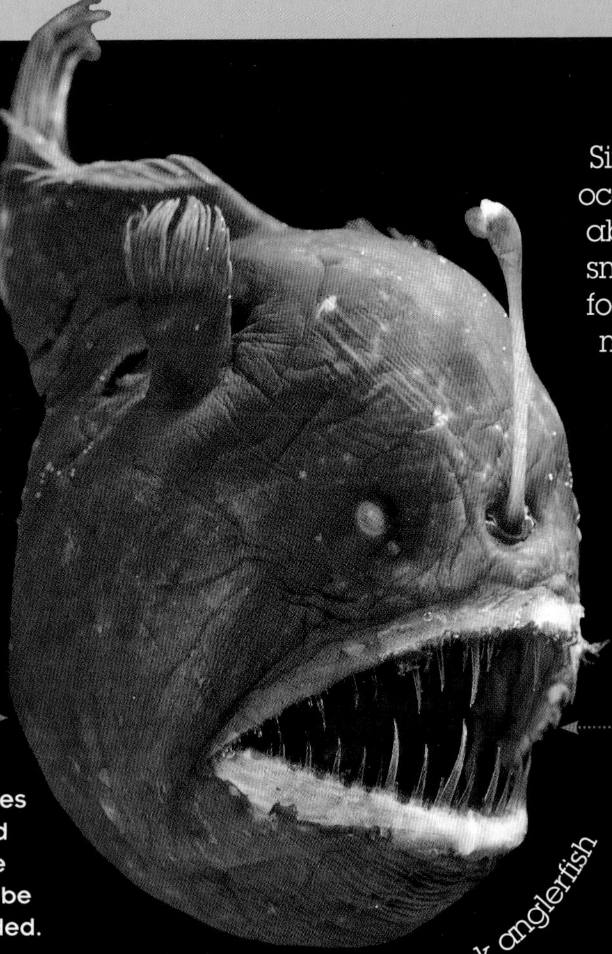

Since its bones are thin and flexible, the stomach can be greatly extended.

This anglerfish's huge mouth and long teeth enable it to eat prey larger than itself.

Humpback anglerfish

Giant hatchetfish

The eyes are positioned to look upward for the shapes of prey against the faint light.

The largest ocean hatchetfish, this fish reaches only 11 cm (4.3 in) long.

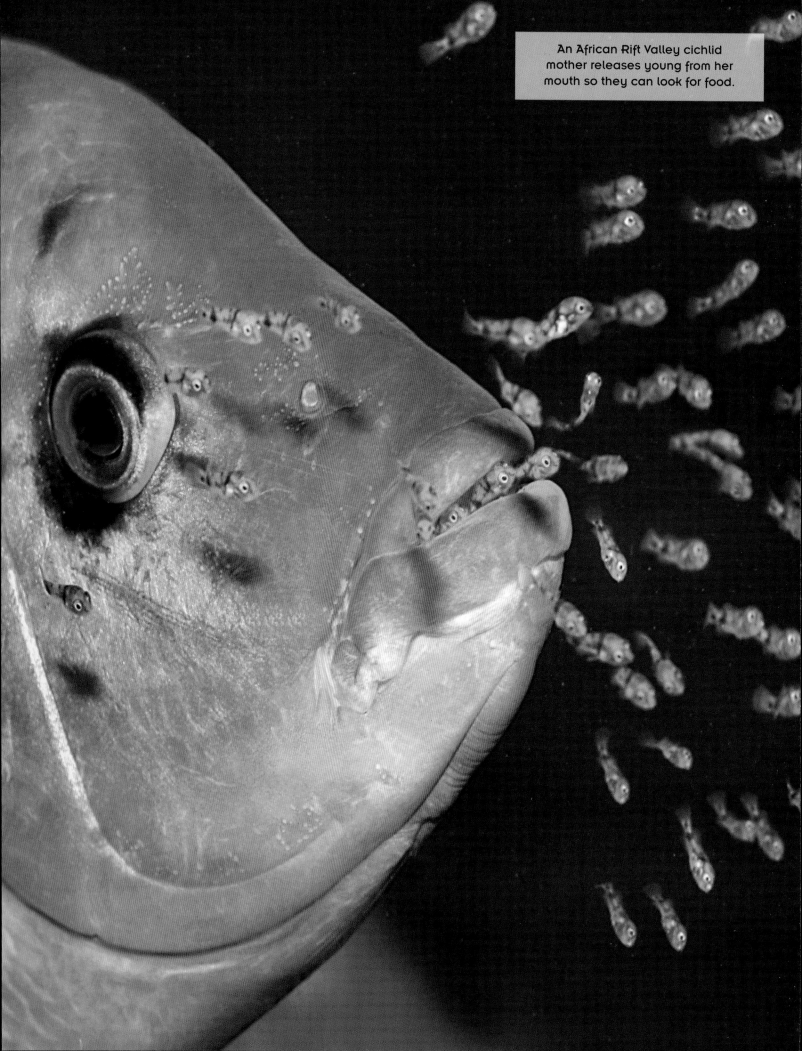

An African Rift Valley cichlid mother releases young from her mouth so they can look for food.

CICHLIDS

There are at least 1,600 species of cichlids, with more discovered every year. The majority of fish abandon their eggs and take no care of their young. Cichlid parents are unusual because they guard their eggs and then take care of young for several weeks or months.

Some cichlids lay eggs in a crevice or shell, among plants, or in a pit dug in the mud or sand using the mouth. After the female lays her eggs, the male usually guards the nest from intruders. Using her fins, the female fans water over the eggs to keep them supplied with oxygen. After the eggs hatch, the young are cared for by the mother, father, both parents, or even groups of parents that share the work. Some parents dig at the sand, raising tiny animals for their young to eat, while others catch food then chew it for their babies. Some species dig new pits to accommodate their babies as they grow.

Other cichlids are mouthbrooders, with females holding eggs or young in the safety of their mouth. Some females scoop their eggs into their mouth as soon as they are laid, while others lay their eggs in a pit or crevice then gulp the young when they hatch. The babies are released to look for food under the care of the mother, with the father usually playing no part.

A South American cichlid, the oscar lays up to 3,000 eggs on a flat rock after rubbing against it for several days to make sure it is clean. Young are cared for until they are almost a year old.

Family:	Cichlidae
Range:	Tropical and subtropical Africa, Asia, and the Americas
Habitat:	Lakes, rivers, and occasionally coastal oceans
Diet:	Algae, plants, fish, invertebrates, and waste
Size:	2–90 cm (0.8–35 in) long

Neolamprologus multifasciatus

Giant cichlid

Chapter 7

INVERTEBRATES

Around 97 percent of animals are invertebrates, which share the feature of not having a backbone. Yet while some are entirely soft-bodied, others have a hard shell. Some have a brain, but others do not. They may have no legs or up to 750, like an *Illacme* millipede.

There are more than 30 phyla, or groups, of invertebrates. The largest phyla include arthropods, mollusks, cnidarians, echinoderms, nematodes, and porifera.

Arthropods are the most common animals of all, with at least 1 million species and perhaps ten times that number still to be identified. Arthropods include insects; arachnids, such as spiders; myriapods, such as millipedes; and crustaceans, such as crabs. Arthropods have a segmented body with a tough covering called an exoskeleton, as well as paired, jointed legs. Insects are the largest group of arthropods. They have a three-part body, six legs, and a pair of antennae, or feelers.

Mollusks include cephalopods, such as octopus and squid; bivalves, including clams and mussels; and gastropods, such as slugs and snails. Mollusks have a soft, unsegmented body with a muscly covering called a mantle and sometimes a hard shell. Cnidarians, such as corals, are water-dwellers with stinging cells. Echinoderms, including starfish (also called sea stars) and sea urchins, are found only in the ocean. Nematodes are worms, while porifera are simple, brainless, water-dwelling animals known as sponges.

A member of the insect class, the spiny flower mantis has four walking legs and two large forelegs for grabbing prey.

Like all millipedes, the Siamese pointy-tailed millipede has two pairs of jointed legs on most body segments.

Skeletons

While invertebrates do not have backbones, they do have a non-bony skeleton that supports their body, either inside or out, and helps movement. Arthropods have an external skeleton, called an exoskeleton, made largely from a strong but bendy material called chitin. Some gastropods have a shell rich in the hard mineral calcium, which is also found in vertebrate bones. Echinoderms have an internal skeleton of calcium-rich plates. Earthworms and jellyfish have skeletons made of compartments filled with watery fluid.

Not a true crab, a hermit crab is an arthropod that lives in a discarded mollusk shell to protect its soft exoskeleton.

BEETLES

Around 400,000 species of beetles have been discovered, making up a quarter of all known animals. Like all insects, beetles have a three-part body: the head, holding the brain; the thorax, to which the legs and wings are joined; and the abdomen, containing the stomach and heart.

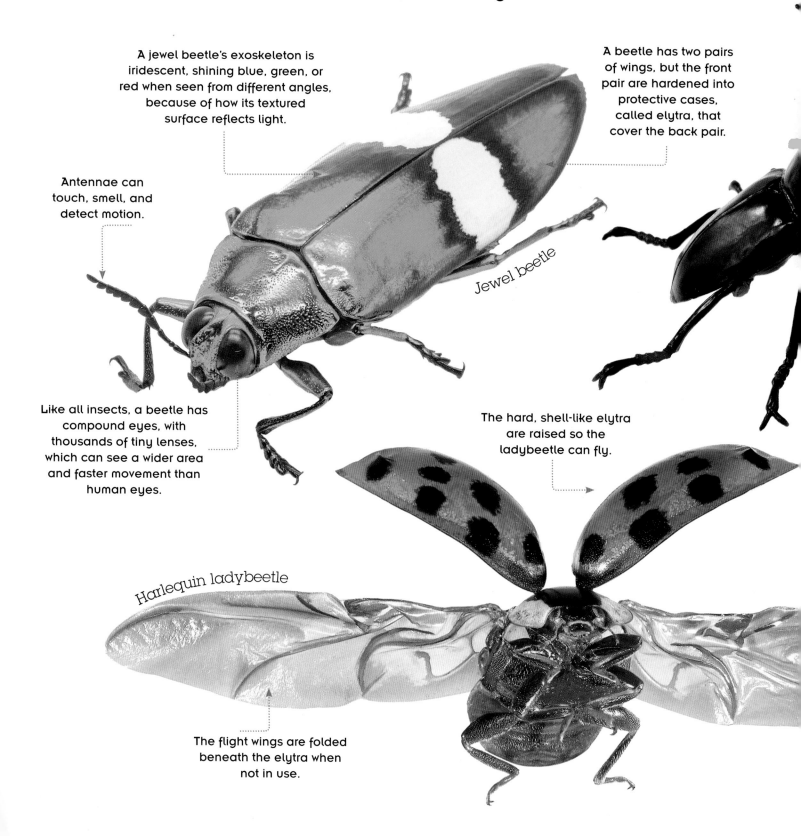

A jewel beetle's exoskeleton is iridescent, shining blue, green, or red when seen from different angles, because of how its textured surface reflects light.

A beetle has two pairs of wings, but the front pair are hardened into protective cases, called elytra, that cover the back pair.

Antennae can touch, smell, and detect motion.

Jewel beetle

Like all insects, a beetle has compound eyes, with thousands of tiny lenses, which can see a wider area and faster movement than human eyes.

The hard, shell-like elytra are raised so the ladybeetle can fly.

Harlequin ladybeetle

The flight wings are folded beneath the elytra when not in use.

Male stag beetles fight with their enlarged mouthparts, called mandibles, which can also be used for grabbing food.

This beetle eats the leaves, stems, and flowers of plants in the lily family.

Scarlet lily beetle

A beetle larva will go through dramatic body changes, called complete metamorphosis, as it becomes an adult.

Dung beetle larvae

European stag beetle

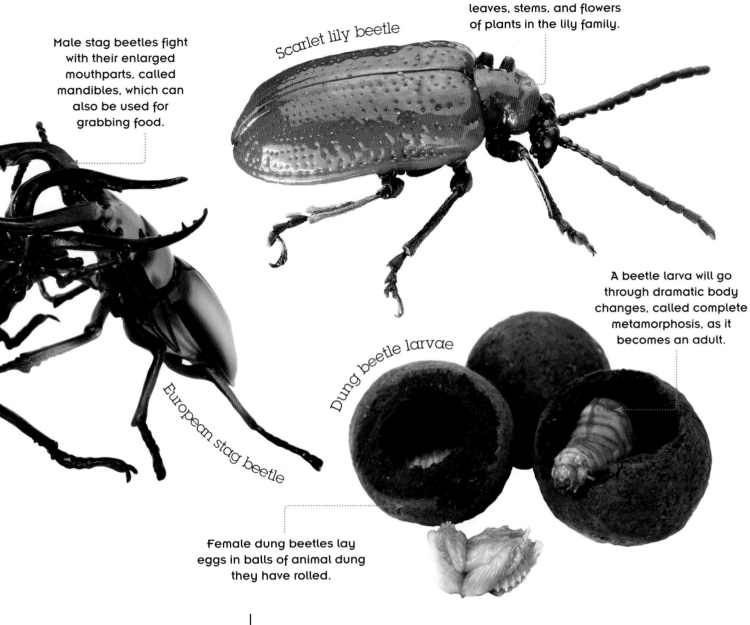

Female dung beetles lay eggs in balls of animal dung they have rolled.

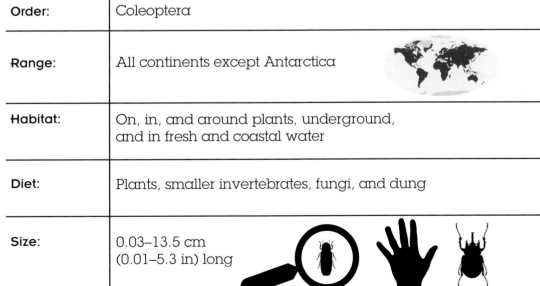

Order:	Coleoptera
Range:	All continents except Antarctica
Habitat:	On, in, and around plants, underground, and in fresh and coastal water
Diet:	Plants, smaller invertebrates, fungi, and dung
Size:	0.03–13.5 cm (0.01–5.3 in) long

Scydosella beetle

Actaeon beetle

Found in North Africa, Europe, and northern Asia, the adult common blue butterfly lives for only three weeks.

BUTTERFLIES

When adult, these insects flutter from flower to flower on their four, scale-covered wings. These are patterned for camouflage or in bright shades to warn predators that the butterfly tastes nasty. Butterflies start life as wingless, long-bodied larvae called caterpillars.

Butterflies go through complete metamorphosis. They have a four-stage life cycle: egg, larva, pupa, and adult. Females usually lay eggs on the plant their caterpillars will eat. Most caterpillars have six true legs and extra, fleshy "prolegs." They have strong mandibles for chewing. As caterpillars get bigger, they shed their outgrown exoskeleton several times.

After a few weeks, caterpillars shed their last exoskeleton to reveal a hard skin called a chrysalis, which they attach to a branch with silk. Inside their chrysalis, caterpillars pupate, or change into an adult. After a week or two, or perhaps a whole winter, the chrysalis splits open. Adult butterflies have a long, tubelike mouthpart, called a proboscis, which they use for sucking liquid food, such as flower nectar. Adult butterflies live for a few weeks or months.

Butterflies are closely related to moths. Although there are exceptions, butterflies usually have club-shaped antennae, while those of moths are feathery or threadlike. When at rest, butterflies normally fold their wings in an upright position, while most moths hold them horizontally.

The chocolate albatross sucks up nutrients from wet soil and rotting plants.

Suborder:	Rhopalocera
Range:	All continents except Antarctica
Habitat:	Around flowering plants in habitats from rain forest to desert
Diet:	As adults, nectar, tree sap, rotting plants, dung, and minerals in mud
Size:	1.2–28 cm (0.5–11 in) wingspan

Western pygmy blue

Queen Alexandra's birdwing

BEES AND WASPS

These winged insects have a proboscis for drinking nectar and other liquids. At the tip of their abdomen, females have a long tubelike organ called an ovipositor, which is used for laying eggs and, in many species, for stinging. Male wasps and bees cannot sting.

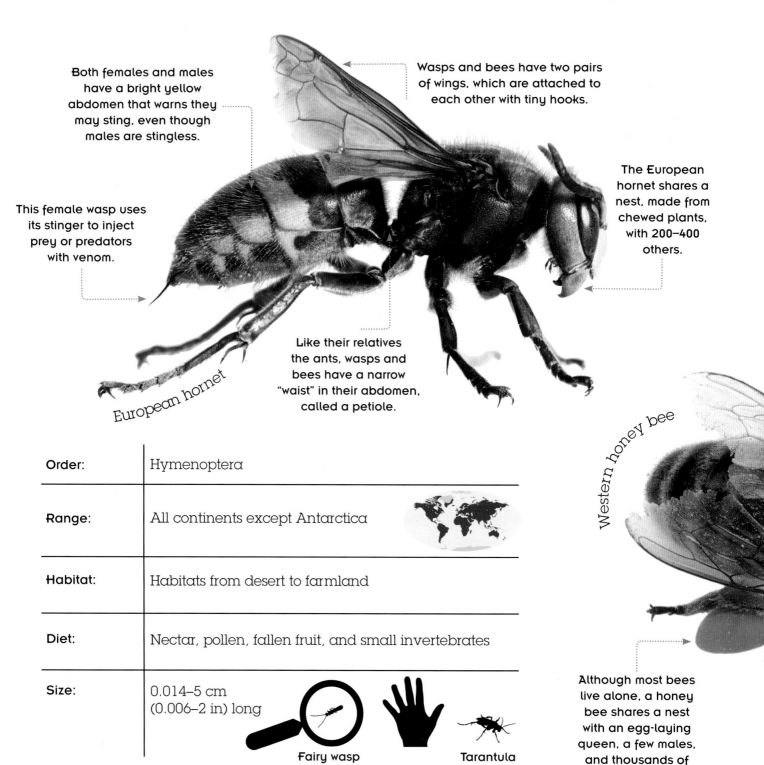

Both females and males have a bright yellow abdomen that warns they may sting, even though males are stingless.

Wasps and bees have two pairs of wings, which are attached to each other with tiny hooks.

This female wasp uses its stinger to inject prey or predators with venom.

The European hornet shares a nest, made from chewed plants, with 200–400 others.

Like their relatives the ants, wasps and bees have a narrow "waist" in their abdomen, called a petiole.

European hornet

Western honey bee

Order:	Hymenoptera
Range:	All continents except Antarctica
Habitat:	Habitats from desert to farmland
Diet:	Nectar, pollen, fallen fruit, and small invertebrates
Size:	0.014–5 cm (0.006–2 in) long

Fairy wasp

Tarantula hawk wasp

Although most bees live alone, a honey bee shares a nest with an egg-laying queen, a few males, and thousands of female "workers."

Potter wasp

Like most wasps, the potter wasp is solitary, building its own nest in which to lay a single egg.

The nest is made from mud mixed with water that the wasp has drunk then spat back up.

This female wasp has paralyzed a caterpillar with her sting and is leaving it for her larva to eat.

In hairy cavities on its hindlegs, the honey bee collects flower pollen, which will be stored as food for the hive.

This wasp lays eggs in another wasp's nest, then its larvae eat the other wasp's eggs or larvae.

Ruby tailed wasp

Buff-tailed bumblebee

It drinks flower nectar using its long proboscis tipped with a hairy tongue, called a glossa.

Pollen is carried on its hair from flower to flower, enabling them to produce seeds.

CRABS

There are over 6,000 species of true crabs. A crab's extremely hard exoskeleton is often called a shell. A crab must shed its exoskeleton as it grows bigger, revealing a new, softer shell underneath.

Along with lobsters, prawns, and shrimp, crabs belong to a group of arthropods called decapods (meaning "ten legs") because they have ten walking legs. In crabs, the front pair of legs has pincers that are used for catching and crushing prey. Pincers may also be used for communicating, by drumming or waving, and for fighting over mates or hiding places. Crabs also have two pairs of antennae and a pair of eyes, which may be on stalks. Decapods are part of the crustacean group, which also includes woodlice and barnacles. All crustaceans have a hard exoskeleton over their segmented body.

Most crabs can only walk sideways, due to the way in which their jointed legs can bend. However, some walk forward or backward. Swimming crabs may have a back pair of legs that are flattened into a paddle-like shape.

Some crabs live entirely in water, some move between water and land, and some are purely land-living. Crabs have gills, which are able to take oxygen from water. On land, as long as these special gills stay damp, they can take oxygen from the air.

A male fiddler crab has one pincer much larger than the other. It uses the larger pincer for fighting other males and for communication.

Infraorder:	Brachyura
Range:	All oceans plus tropical and subtropical regions of land
Habitat:	Oceans, freshwater, land, and inside other animals
Diet:	Algae, invertebrates, fungi, and waste
Size:	1 cm–3.7 m (2.5 in–12.1 ft) long

Pea crab

Japanese spider crab

Every year, millions of Christmas Island red crabs migrate from Christmas Island's forests to the beach, where they will mate.

FOCUS ON:

ARACHNIDS

Spiders, scorpions, and ticks are arachnids. Their body is in two parts: cephalothorax and abdomen. Their eight legs are attached to the cephalothorax. The cephalothorax also has chelicerae, which are jawlike mouthparts, and pedipalps, which can help with feeding or walking.

There are nearly 50,000 species of spiders. Their chelicerae are equipped with hollow fangs that can inject venom to paralyze or kill prey. On their abdomens, they have silk-making glands called spinnerets. Silk can be used for tasks such as making webs and wrapping eggs. Nearly all spiders are meat-eaters, with small species eating invertebrates and large ones sometimes eating birds or lizards. While many spiders trap prey in sticky webs, others catch prey by running, swinging a thread of sticky silk, or suddenly jumping out of a burrow.

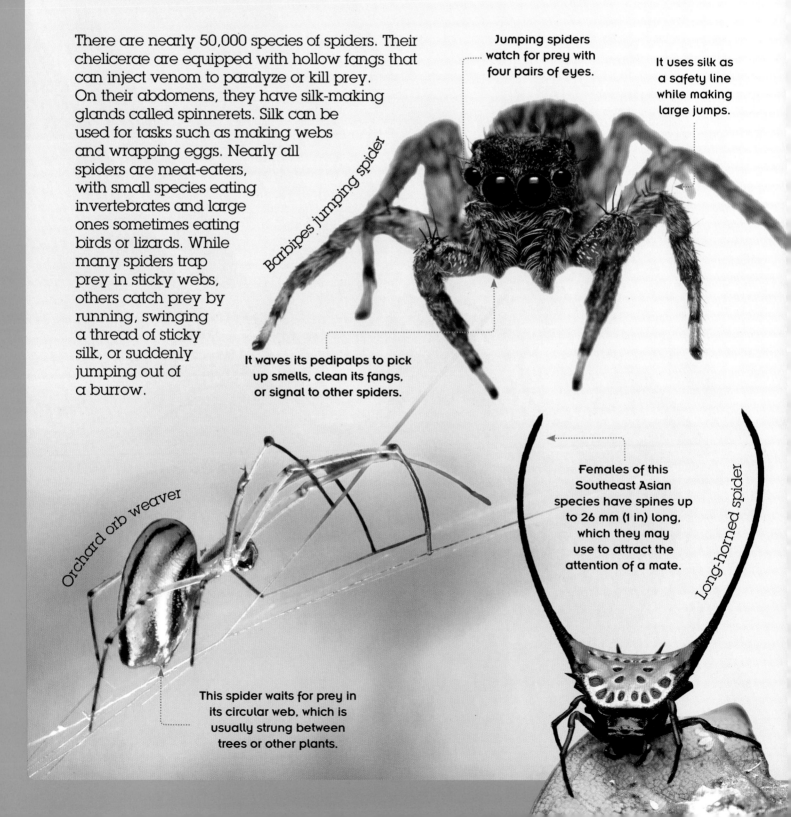

Jumping spiders watch for prey with four pairs of eyes.

It uses silk as a safety line while making large jumps.

Barbipes jumping spider

It waves its pedipalps to pick up smells, clean its fangs, or signal to other spiders.

Orchard orb weaver

This spider waits for prey in its circular web, which is usually strung between trees or other plants.

Females of this Southeast Asian species have spines up to 26 mm (1 in) long, which they may use to attract the attention of a mate.

Long-horned spider

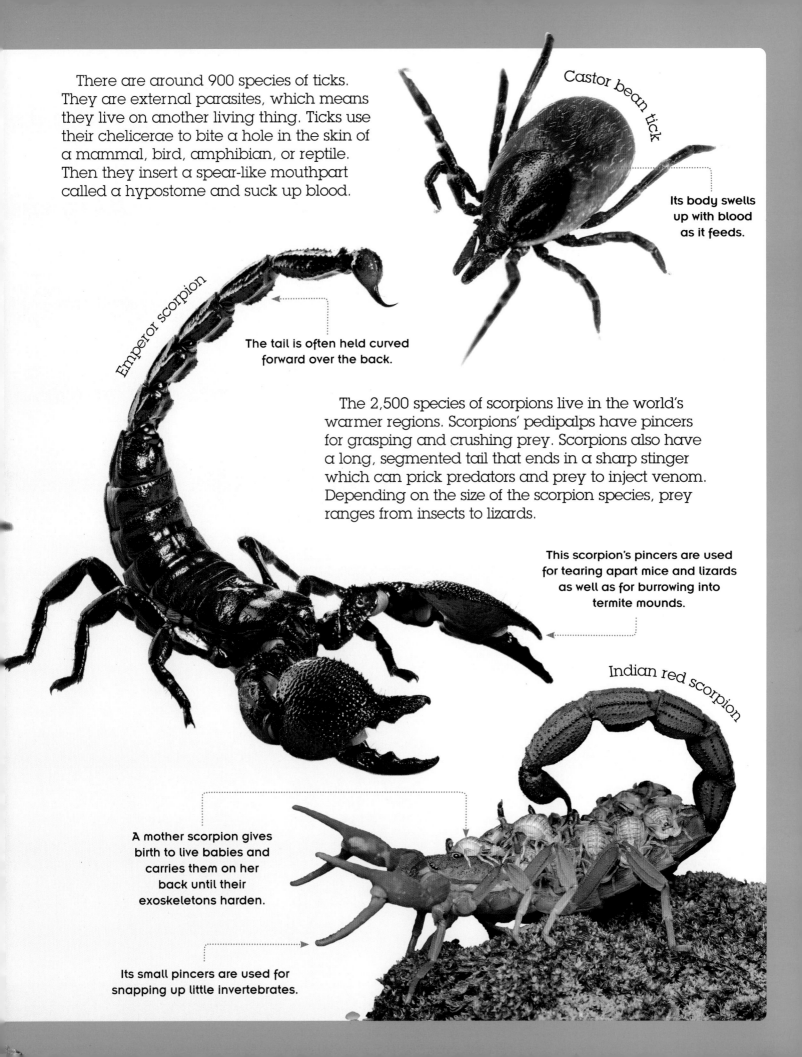

There are around 900 species of ticks. They are external parasites, which means they live on another living thing. Ticks use their chelicerae to bite a hole in the skin of a mammal, bird, amphibian, or reptile. Then they insert a spear-like mouthpart called a hypostome and suck up blood.

Castor bean tick

Its body swells up with blood as it feeds.

Emperor scorpion

The tail is often held curved forward over the back.

The 2,500 species of scorpions live in the world's warmer regions. Scorpions' pedipalps have pincers for grasping and crushing prey. Scorpions also have a long, segmented tail that ends in a sharp stinger which can prick predators and prey to inject venom. Depending on the size of the scorpion species, prey ranges from insects to lizards.

This scorpion's pincers are used for tearing apart mice and lizards as well as for burrowing into termite mounds.

Indian red scorpion

A mother scorpion gives birth to live babies and carries them on her back until their exoskeletons harden.

Its small pincers are used for snapping up little invertebrates.

The bright, contrasting pattern of the nembrothine sea slug warns predators that it contains venom, which it gets from eating and storing the stinging cells of jellyfish.

SLUGS AND SNAILS

Slugs and snails live in oceans, in freshwater, and on land. They make up the gastropod (meaning "stomach foot") group of mollusks. There are at least 65,000 gastropod species. Snails have a shell into which they can pull their soft body, but slugs do not.

Gastropods have one or two pairs of tentacles on their head. The tentacles are able to feel, smell, and taste. Gastropods also have eyes, usually at the tips of their tentacles or at their bases. Most gastropod eyes are simple, seeing only light and dark. Gastropods do not have true brains, but they do have collections of nerve cells that co-ordinate responses to their surroundings.

Slugs and snails have a tongue-like mouthpart called a radula, which is armed with tiny teeth. While plant-eaters use their radula for scraping algae off rocks, meat-eaters may use it for boring through shells or injecting venom.

A gastropod's head is joined to its long "foot." Land-living gastropods move by making wavelike motions with their foot, which pushes them forward. They also produce slimy mucus to make the ground slippery and easier to slide across. Swimming gastropods move by waving their entire foot or flaplike portions of it. Some gastropods, such as limpets, do not often move. They use their strong, muscly foot to cling to rocks on the seashore.

Like most snails, the garden snail has a spiral shell with an opening on its right-hand side.

Class:	Gastropoda
Range:	All oceans and all continents except Antarctica
Habitat:	Oceans, freshwater, and land
Diet:	Algae, fungi, waste, plants, mollusks, worms, and fish
Size:	0.1–99 cm (0.04–39 in) long

Omalogyridae sea snail

Australian trumpet sea snail

OCTOPUS

Octopus have eight limbs, two eyes, and a mouth with a sharp, hard beak. Their soft body can be flattened and stretched, so it can squeeze into crevices. Along with their relatives the cuttlefish, octopus have the largest brains compared to body size of all invertebrates.

Octopus are ocean-dwelling mollusks. Along with squid, cuttlefish, and nautiluses, they are in the cephalopod (meaning "head-feet") group, known for their large heads. Octopus are among the most intelligent invertebrates. They reveal this in how they communicate with each other, by spreading their limbs and changing their skin shade. They also have complex survival strategies. For example, the mimic octopus moves its body and limbs to pretend to be other animals, such as lionfish and sea snakes, so it can avoid predators or catch prey.

When most octopus need to move fast, they suck water inside their muscly body wall, called a mantle, then squeeze it out through a funnel-like body part called a siphon. This jet creates a backward force, which pushes them forward. Octopus can also crawl along the ocean bottom. They push and pull themselves over the rock or mud using their arms, which have sticky suckers on the underside.

Most octopus have an ink sac, which can spray out dark ink mixed with mucus when the octopus is threatened. In a cloud of ink, a predator cannot see the octopus as it swims away.

When the blue-ringed octopus is threatened, its rings glow to warn predators that it is venomous.

Order:	Octopoda
Range:	All oceans
Habitat:	Coastal waters to the deepest ocean trenches
Diet:	Crustaceans, worms, mollusks, and fish
Size:	2.5 cm–4.3 m (1 in–14 ft) arm span

Star-sucker pygmy octopus

Giant Pacific octopus

The coconut octopus collects coconut and mollusk shells, then uses them to hide inside or build a den.

CNIDARIANS

Cnidarians include corals, jellyfish, and sea anemones. There are over 11,000 species of cnidarians, living in oceans and in freshwater. They are fairly simple animals with no true brain. They use special stinging cells to capture prey.

Cnidarians have only one opening in their body, which is used for eating and excreting, or pooping. Around this opening are tentacles, armed with stinging cells that fire harpoon-like structures that pierce and poison small prey. The tentacles then pass prey to the mouth. Some cnidarians—such as corals and the Portuguese man o' war—live in colonies, or large groups, with others of their species.

A gas-filled sac floats at the water surface, letting the colony drift with the winds and currents.

Portuguese man o' war

Although it looks like a jellyfish, the Portuguese man o' war is actually a colony of many tiny medusas and polyps.

One sea fan coral is composed of thousands of eight-tentacled polyps.

Sea fan

Cnidarians have two main body forms: medusa and polyp. Medusae, shaped like umbrellas with their tentacles dangling downward, can swim slowly through the water. Polyps have cylinder-shaped bodies and tentacles that point upward. They are usually sessile, or non-moving, remaining firmly attached to a solid surface. Some cnidarians, including jellyfish, are polyps when young, then mature into medusae. However, corals and sea anemones are sessile polyps when adults.

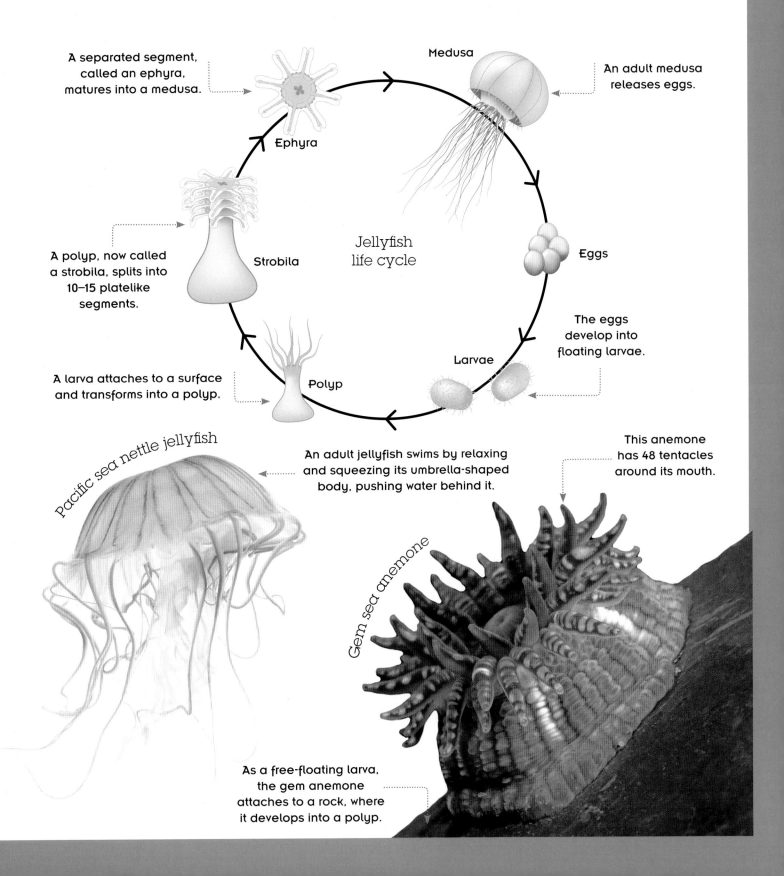

A separated segment, called an ephyra, matures into a medusa.

Medusa

An adult medusa releases eggs.

Ephyra

A polyp, now called a strobila, splits into 10–15 platelike segments.

Strobila

Jellyfish life cycle

Eggs

The eggs develop into floating larvae.

A larva attaches to a surface and transforms into a polyp.

Polyp

Larvae

Pacific sea nettle jellyfish

An adult jellyfish swims by relaxing and squeezing its umbrella-shaped body, pushing water behind it.

This anemone has 48 tentacles around its mouth.

Gem sea anemone

As a free-floating larva, the gem anemone attaches to a rock, where it develops into a polyp.

In the shallow waters of the Pacific Ocean, a small rainbow star is regenerating three damaged arms.

STARFISH

Also known as sea stars, starfish live on the ocean floor, from shallow coastal waters to the deep sea. Starfish are radially symmetrical, which means their bodies form a repeating pattern around a central point.

Starfish have arms that radiate, or spread, from a central disk. While many starfish have five arms, some have as many as fifty. A starfish's underside has many tube feet, which work like tiny suckers, sticking to the ocean floor or rocks. By pressing down one arm and lifting another, a starfish crawls along.

A starfish's mouth is on the underside of its central disk. Many species are able to climb on top of prey, then push their stomach out through their mouth, covering the animal. In the case of two-shelled mollusks such as clams, the starfish squeezes part of its stomach in between the two shells. The stomach then releases fluid that starts to digest, or break down, the prey. The stomach and mushy food is then pulled back inside the disk.

When caught by a predator, some starfish can shed an arm, by quickly softening their body tissues. Over the course of several months, they can then regenerate, or regrow, the damaged arm. A few starfish can regenerate their central disk even if all that remains of their body is one arm.

Starfish soak up oxygen from the water through their tube feet and tiny bumps, called papulae, on their skin. They are often found in tide pools, where they are able to survive short periods out of water at low tide due to their thick skin.

The common sunstar has between eight and fourteen arms. Its upper surface is covered with protective spines.

Class:	Asteroidea
Range:	All oceans
Habitat:	Ocean floor from deep sea to coral reefs and tide pools
Diet:	Algae, sponges, sea urchins, mollusks, corals, and waste
Size:	1 cm–1 m (0.4–39 in) arm span

Parvulastra starfish

Sunflower sea star

GLOSSARY

ABDOMEN The back part of an insect's body.

ALGAE Plantlike living things that live in and around water, such as seaweeds.

AMPHIBIAN An animal that usually spends part of its life on land and part in water.

ARACHNID An invertebrate with eight legs and a body in two parts.

ARTHROPOD An invertebrate with a hard covering, or exoskeleton, and jointed legs, such as an insect, arachnid, or crab.

BASK To rest in the sunshine.

BIRD An animal with a beak, wings, and feathers.

BRACKISH Slightly salty water.

CAMOUFLAGE The way the shade and shape of an animal make it less visible in its habitat.

CANINE A pointed tooth between the front teeth (incisors) and back teeth (premolars) of a mammal.

CELL The smallest working part of an animal's body.

CEPHALOTHORAX The joined head and thorax of spiders, scorpions, ticks, and crabs.

CHROMATOPHORE A cell containing pigment.

CNIDARIAN A water-living invertebrate with stinging cells.

COMPOUND EYE An eye containing many small lenses.

CRITICALLY ENDANGERED Describes a species that is at high risk of soon becoming extinct.

DOMESTIC Tame and kept by humans.

ECHOLOCATION A process for locating objects by making sounds and detecting their echo.

ENDANGERED Describes a species that is likely to become extinct in the near future.

ESTUARY A body of coastal water where freshwater from rivers and streams mixes with saltwater from the ocean.

EVOLVE To change gradually over time.

EXOSKELETON The hard outer covering of some invertebrates.

FAMILY A group of species that are closely related, so they look and behave quite alike. For example, lions and tigers are in the cat family.

FISH A water-living animal that takes oxygen from the water using gills and usually has fins.

FRESHWATER Unsalted water such as rivers, lakes, and ponds.

GILL An organ that takes oxygen from water.

GLAND A body part that makes a substance for use in the body or for release.

HABITAT The natural home of an animal, plant, or other living thing.

HEMISPHERE Half of the planet, such as the northern or southern half on either side of the equator.

INCISOR A tooth at the front of the mouth in a mammal.

INSECT An invertebrate with six legs and a three-part body: head, thorax, and abdomen.

INVERTEBRATE An animal without a backbone, such as a crab, octopus, or insect.

KRILL A small, shrimplike invertebrate.

LARVA A young stage in the life cycle of some invertebrates, fish, and amphibians, during which the animal looks different from its adult form.

LUNG An organ that takes oxygen from air.

MAMMAL An animal that grows hair at some point in its life and feeds its young on milk.

MANDIBLE A jaw or jawlike mouthpart, usually used for biting.

MARSH An area of land that is flooded for part of the year.

METAMORPHOSIS The change in body shape that amphibians and some invertebrates and fish go through as they grow into adults.

MOLLUSK An invertebrate with a soft body and sometimes a hard shell, such as a slug, snail, or octopus.

MUCUS A slimy substance made by some animals.

NECTAR A sugary liquid made by flowers.

NOCTURNAL Active at night.

NUTRIENT A substance needed by an animal's body for growth and health.

ORDER A group of families that are closely related. For example, the cat and dog families are in the meat-eating Carnivora order.

OXYGEN A gas found in air and water that is needed by animals' cells for making energy.

PIGMENT A material that creates hue, such as red or blue.

POLLEN A powder made by flowers. It can fertilize other flowers of the same species so that they make seeds.

PROBOSCIS The long, sucking mouthpart of an insect.

RANGE The area where an animal is found.

REPTILE An animal with a dry skin, covered in scales or scutes, that usually lays eggs on land.

SCALE A small, hard plate that protects the skin of most fish and some reptiles.

SCUTE A bony plate with a horny covering.

SEGMENT A division of an animal's body or body part.

SHRUBLAND An area where most plants are shrubs or bushes.

SPECIES A group of living things that look similar and can mate together.

SUBTROPICAL In the areas to the south or north of the tropics, where it is fairly warm all year.

TEMPERATE In the areas between the subtropics and polar regions, where the temperature ranges from cold to warm.

THORAX The middle part of an insect's body. The legs are attached to the thorax.

TROPICAL In the area around the equator, where it is hot all year.

TUNDRA A cold region of treeless ground.

VENOM A poison made by an animal.

VERTEBRATE An animal with a backbone, such as a mammal, bird, fish, amphibian, or reptile.

WEBBED FEET Having toes that are linked by tissue and skin, making them paddle-like.

WINGSPAN The distance across the wings, measuring from wingtip to wingtip.

INDEX